# Now You Must Dance

# NOW YOU MUST DANCE

BRUCE LEEMING

SCOTTISH CULTURAL PRESS

First published 1996
Scottish Cultural Press
Unit 14 Leith Walk Business Centre, 130 Leith Walk,
Edinburgh EH6 5DT
Tel: 0131 555 5950 • Fax: 0131 555 5018

**British Library Cataloguing in Publication Data**
A catalogue record for this book is available
from the British Library

ISBN: 1 898218 71 4

Printed by
Cromwell Press, Melksham, Wiltshire

While some of the characters in this novel contain elements of people I have had to do with over the years, none is wholly based on any specific individual I have ever known.

## ACKNOWLEDGEMENTS

For their encouragement and practical assistance I must thank Sir Ludovic Kennedy, J. Derrick McClure at the University of Aberdeen, my agent Eleanor Milne, the poet Kenneth C. Steven, Nigel Dewar Gibb and William Warren, friends from my youth, and, not least, my wife Dorothy.

To leal Scots, everywhere

*I have brought you to the ring and now you must dance*

Sir William Wallace to his men before the Battle of Falkirk, 1298.

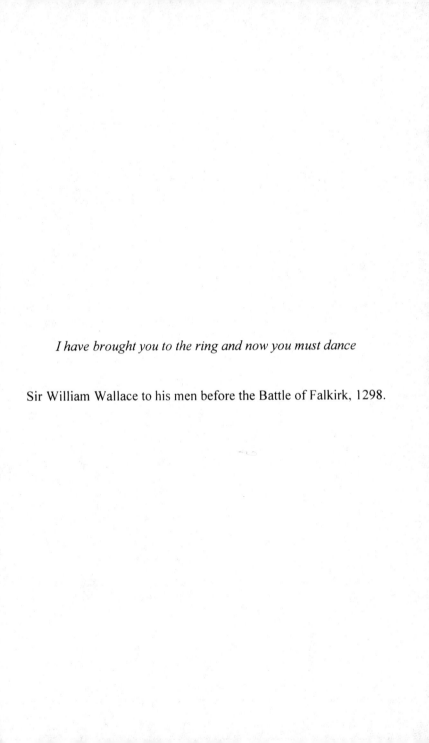

# ONE

WELCOME TO SCOTLAND. James Ballantyne silenced the hard rock cassette which had been thumping his thoughts to a comfortable numbness since somewhere in the Lake District. He let out a prolonged whoop in the company Mercedes as the Tourist Board roadsign receded behind him, his habit whenever he crossed the Border from the south. It was a shout of happiness.

Apart from short visits, he'd been away from the country of his birth and upbringing for six years now. It was a great opportunity he was coming back to in 1995, but with Father gone and Mum now settled down in Hampstead with Aunt Jen things were going to be different. For a moment, as he entered the bleak Southern Uplands, his stomach contracted nervously. But then he yelled again, robustly cheerful. All his memories of Scotland were good. He was only 26 and a highly presentable specimen, if he said it himself, and with a terrific future. He took the six cylinder Merc up to an effortless 100mph on the invitingly empty motorway.

Jamie was a free agent, not least in the girlie stakes now that Caroline Courtney had finally bitten the dust. Christ, what a caper that had been. They'd laughed a lot together, enjoyed discos and good eating in neat bistros – all that big city stuff. And the less said the better about the infinite variety of their bedtime games: no shadow of doubt, they were eminently compatible in that department! But in the end it became obvious that sexy Caro was plain thick. If he raised any serious topic – politics, maybe trends in modern art, her immediate reaction was to attempt to divert attention from the aching acres of her ignorance by pulling his trousers down.

However, this expedient could not be relied upon in public places, so they'd started arguing, then quarrelling, then lapsing into painful silences. Truthfully, they'd both been mightily relieved to call it a day.

Before that there had been Nadine in New York, from the Creative Division. Once or twice a week regularly for about six months they'd given one another joy back in her apartment, until he'd discovered that Ms Nadine apparently saw no conflict of interest in making another good friend equally joyful on her evenings off from him. His recall of dealings with the opposite sex before Nadine tended to merge into a vague, perfumed amorphism. Nothing serious. Except for Gillian MacIntyre.

Jamie called the Automobile Club in Glasgow on the carphone to tell them he'd be early and to make sure his room was ready.

He'd known Gill for ever. As tinies they'd attended Miss Patterson-White's kindergarten near their homes in Bearsden, to the west of Glasgow. Although he was actually of an age with Gill's sister Fiona, who was older by two years, he'd seemed from the beginning to take to Gill. Later on, when he'd gone off to boarding school, contact was maintained during the holidays. They'd not gone out together, on their own, until after school, and then only a few times for a run in his second-hand banger or to the cinema. Jamie's main recollection of those occasions was one of acute sexual frustration and confined-space discomfort. They'd really been incredibly innocent. Then Gill went to university and he joined the *Scottish Field* magazine as a trainee in the advertising department. They drifted apart. A year later Jamie was in London with Mekay & Schwartz, an American company offering training in New York.

During visits home in subsequent years he hadn't failed to observe the burgeoning beauty of his childhood friend. Gill was no longer just an attractive girl – she had developed into a most desirable young lady. Tallish, there was an alluring womanliness about her too. Her skin was fine, faintly olive with a pink underglow, her thick fair hair bounced, her teeth were even and her eyes, brown with green points, shone with amused intelligence. As he entered the last lap of the journey to Glasgow, Jamie determined to look up Gill MacIntyre before many more days passed.

Wow! She'd make some lover! But a good brain too. They could talk sensibly. They'd be quite a couple. His mind raced ahead, exciting thoughts jostling. He was going to find a flat in the West End. Gill and he could have friends in for chic little dinner parties. Maybe they could take a holiday together soon in the Caribbean or the South of France. Was she still living at home? Her parents were friendly enough folks, but Gill might well be finding life in Muirlaw Drive rather dull by now. And might she be involved with someone else? Never mind – he'd soon see off any competition.


Gill had known Willie Devine for a couple of months now. She'd not long started in her first teaching job when they'd met. It was a tough Secondary in the insalubrious Partick district and she'd been taken aback more than once by the unselfconscious use of thoroughly bad language by her twelve year old charges. "Shut yer fuckin' hole, Kevin!" or, "Piss off, y'durty hoor, Senga," she'd had to accept as standard playground badinage. But as she became familiar with the children's individual personalities she warmed to them. It was easy to see that their home backgrounds were rarely conducive to the idea that school instruction be taken seriously. However, some of them *did* want to learn, and it was a delight to furnish their receptive young minds with knowledge and new ideas.

Gill's staff colleagues were a mixed bunch, some cynical and bored, irritated by constant policy shifts in regard to the curriculum. Others were birds of passage, temporary supply-teachers, professional, uncommunicative. A few were quite friendly, even prepared to overlook her comfortable upbringing and 'fancy' education. She teamed up with Sally Hughes, John MacAslan and Cathie Lonie, who were all in their twenties too. They chatted together in the staffroom over paper cups of execrable coffee and lunchtime sandwiches. There many a giggle. One Friday evening, after an internal meeting that had gone on a bit, John suggested the four of them go for a drink. He took them into The Argyle in Dumbarton Road.

This was an aggressively traditional pub, without benefit of stainless steel and plastic gimcrackery. Its high, nicotine-stained plaster-moulded ceiling, its purple flock-clad walls and its dark mahogany and brass bar furniture were meant for drinking amongst first, and only secondly as a venue for socialising. Near the entrance hung a massive faded sepia photograph of the local football team, Partick Thistle, 1921 winners of the Scottish Cup, a worthy group of crop-haired, long-shorted individuals, arms uniformly folded, eyes modestly staring past the camera. The pub's atmosphere was thick with cigarette smoke, redolent of beer and whisky fumes. All around rose and fell the plangent urgencies of Glaswegian working men or, more accurately in many cases, of unemployed Glasgow men in earnest conversation. John found a table for them and went to order drinks. Gill was aware of many curious eyes, but of no slackening in the debates, accompanied by emphatic gestures, around her. Someone touched her elbow.

"Hey, you no wan o' the teacher lassies at the school?"

She turned to see a nondescript individual with a pint of heavy beer in his hand and wearing a camouflage jacket. "Yes ... yes, I'm at ..."

"Thought so. I'm Lex Grant. One of my weans is in yer class – Iain. The wife took me alang to wan o' they parent teacher thingamies a while back. Right?"

"Right. Yes, I know Iain, Mr Grant. He's a bright lad."

"Wee bugger he is."

So saying, this individual jerked his chair back from the table as if to join up the two parties.

"What's yer name again, Miss?"

"Gillian MacIntyre."

"Oh aye, I mind. MacIntyre, aye." He took a thoughtful pull at his beer. "This is Mo Hossein and Willie Devine. Willie's the savvy yin roon these parts. Right, Willie?" He laughed. "This is Julian MacIntyre, guys."

Devine took his cigarette out of his mouth. "How's that? Your first name?" He cocked his head.

"Gillian."

"That's what I telt ye, y'eedjit."

"Uh-huh. OK, Lex. Just checking."

John returned with their drinks on a battered tin tray and introductions were made all round. Fractured conversational exchanges ensued, but any possible common interests were quickly exhausted and the two groups drew apart. Except for Willie and Gill, who moved places so they could talk without shouting.

"I'm usually called Gill."

"Nice," said Willie. "Where're you from?"

"Well, I'm teaching at Rowley Street just along the road, but I live in Bearsden."

He nodded. "My 'bijou apartment' is round the corner in Rubyvale Street." He smiled. "So we're kind of neighbours, Gill."

She smiled back. This character was disconcerting. His eyes, blue-black and frank, seemed to pierce her defences, to search her out.

"Mmm," she replied noncommittally and took a sip of her gin and tonic.

Willie glanced at his watch. "Have to make a move," he remarked.

Gill gave him another friendly smile.

"Got a piece to file about football hooliganism's decline. There's a deadline." He tapped his wrist.

"Are you a journalist then?" Gill enquired.

"Aye. The *Glasgow Recorder*. Ah well, duty calls. Pity – I was just getting interested, weren't you?"

The directness of the question took Gill by surprise. "What? Oh... yes, I was."

"No sweat. I'm in here most nights, so if you've the courage to step into this den of iniquity some other time 'We'll meet again...', as they say in the movies."

"OK, Willie. I'll do that."

"Hey, Lex," he shouted over his shoulder.

"Aye, whit is it, Willie?" came the quick reply.

"I've got tae bugger aff, so take care of this lady. Right?"

"Right, Willie. See ye the morrow night?"

"'Spect so, Lex. *Arrivederci*, one and all."

He departed and a thoughtful Gill MacIntyre was soon on the bus back to Bearsden. Willie Devine looked a highly improbable candidate for friend, and yet she experienced a prompting that they would soon find their lives intertwining. She seemed to have known him all her life somehow. Weird.

Owing to various appointments on both sides it was another ten days before they again found themselves in one another's company. Cathie Lonie had a birthday, so they'd gone to the Argyle for a 'modest celebratory libation' as the pawkie Cathie put it. She'd wanted to go somewhere smarter up in the West End, a wine-bar maybe, but Gill had found herself quietly steering her towards the Argyle.

"Och, come on, Cathie, Sally, the old dump's nearer. My tongue's hanging out!"

There he was, in the same corner with Lex Grant and Mo Hossein. But this time Willie had another companion, a large man with abundant unruly red hair and an equally bushy ginger beard under a straight line of thatched eyebrows. This individual smiled benignly through transparent-framed glasses. The arrivals were greeted by Willie who sang out, "*Three little girls from school are we.*" The two groups joined up and Cathie was duly toasted, again in song.

Hamish MacCorquodale was introduced. He was working in TV, was from the Isle of Lewis and a poet, writing mainly in Gaelic. It transpired that his friend was actually Lex whom, to Gill's growing surprise, she now discovered was also a poet, although in his case the medium was Scots. Lex had evidently recited some of his work on a recent TV programme dealing with the contemporary arts in

Scotland. It was through this that Hamish and he had met.

"Gillian? What a lovely name for a lovely lady. Is that not so, Lex? Just lovely ... Gillian."

The way Hamish pronounced her name, softly, slowly and more like 'Chillian', was almost a caress. Gill fancied she could hear the gentle Atlantic rollers in the subtle cadences of his voice. He was charming.

As usual, the general hubbub made conversation difficult. Nevertheless, Sally, who was taking a night-school course in Gaelic for beginners, soon had Hamish in full spate about the subject clearly closest to his heart, the preservation and extension of his native language. Cathie and Lex seemed to have found something of mutually compelling interest. Gill and Willie picked up easily from their last meeting. Only Mo was rather out of it, but he seemed happily content to fetch drinks for them, to put in the odd quiet comment. Gill wondered about Mo.

Willie said, "Nice to see you. I knew you'd come in again."

"Did you now?" Gill laughed.

"Aye."

There was a short silence between them. He drank deeply from his pint of heavy, but kept his eyes on hers. Gill looked away momentarily, then took a sip from her G & T.

"How did the football article go, Willie? You were rushing to get it in last time."

"OK. I have to put something in about the old 'Fitba' every so often. Maintain the common touch for the *Recorder* readers, you know?"

"So you're not a sports reporter then? Not full time, I mean?"

"Right. I have to cover all sorts in my column."

Gill put her glass down. "Your column?"

"Uh-huh. Have you not seen my byline? Every Wednesday and Saturday."

"Well no, Willie. I must confess ..."

"It's all right, Gill. Bearsden is not exactly our main constituency. More *Herald* and *Daily Telegraph* country out there." He grinned.

"I'll start reading you." Quickly she retreated from a too obviously curious position. "If you recommend it!"

"Cheeky bitch," he said, punching her lightly on the upper arm.

"Tell me, Willie, about the column. What d'you write on mainly?"

"I don't have the title, but I suppose mainly you could call me a 'political commentator'. With special reference to Scottish affairs."

"I see. What sort of angle?"

He drained his glass, removed a ten pound note from his wallet and indicated to the already rising Mo that another round was required.

"Well, Gill, I'm not exactly in the business of praising the Tory non-representatives at Westminster." He paused, eyeing her seriously.

"You support Labour then? The Socialists?"

He rolled a cigarette and lit it. He was not in a hurry to reply. Eventually he said: "I'm not convinced journalists should have over-close party affiliations. People are always trying to pin a label on me, but then ... just when they think they've got me safely pigeonholed, say, as a Labourite ... out I come with an attack on their lukewarm attitudes."

The new drinks were passed out.

"What d'you mean, Willie, 'lukewarm'?"

Lex appeared to have had half an ear to their conversation.

"Those bastarts want it both ways. Cushy jobs down in London *and* control up here. Bloody hypocrites! Scotland's claim of right to independence is just a pain in the neck to those guys." Lex was breathing heavily. His eyes shone.

"Couldn't have put it more succinctly myself, Lex," said Willie with a laugh.

Sally Hughes was a well read, intelligent young woman. "I think there's a lot in what Lex says," she remarked.

Her genial interlocutor, Hamish MacCorquodale, suddenly frowned. "Too true! And some of them would like it fine if the Western Isles just floated away over the horizon, I'm telling you.

Nothing but a damned nuisance needing constant subsidies, in their opinion. And here, those communities should be benefitting *majestically* from oil revenues." Then he said as an afterthought, "And the rest of Scotland."

Willie laughed again. "I'm glad you'll leave something for us poor buggers on the mainland, Hamish! For a wee minute there I thought you had arranged for the relocation of the Hebrides to the North Sea."

This produced general merriment, enjoyed not least by the shaggy Lewisman, whose barking, unexpectedly noisy laugh stopped the gesticulating drinkers at the bar in mid-argument, but only for two or three seconds.

Gill considered the direction of what had been said. She was aware that Willie was covertly watching her as he rolled yet another cigarette.

"You should cut down on those," she said as he recovered from the brief coughing bout which seemed to accompany each new lighting.

"Aye. I know. But I've been at the fags since I was about twelve. Stopped us feeling so hungry."

They looked at one another levelly, without any polite smiles. His eyes were watering slightly. Fleetingly he looked vulnerable.

Gill swallowed discreetly. "From what you're saying, Willie, it seems to me that you have to be a supporter of the SNP. Would *that* be right?"

"The Nationalists say a lot of perfectly sensible and *obvious* things. But I told you, Gill, I consider myself free to comment on *all* ideas. Political proposals by any party. No labels – remember?"

"Yes, I do. Listen, I'd like to get into this a bit farther, but I'll have to go."

"You know where to find me. I'll come prepared for cross-examination next time!" Now they did smile, looking directly into one another's eyes. Gill knew then that she didn't want many days to elapse before they met again. After a few moments he continued, "This is a hell of a place to conduct a dialectical discussion. Would you consider a different venue?"

"Sure, Willie."

"Just the pair of us? Maybe a meal?"

"That'd be nice."

"OK. I'll think of something, Gill."

He reached out and briefly squeezed her hand.

"Chauvinist!" she said. "Maybe *I'll* come up with a suggestion too."

"Good lass! Great," was the enthusiastic reply.

And so it was that next evening they soon left the Argyle and walked northwards into the Hillhead District. There, in a back lane of old-fashioned cobbles, they entered the Paradise Garden Curry House and Take Away, to be greeted by a diminutive, grey-haired Pakistani.

"Welcome, welcome, Mr Willie! and Young Lady! Yes, very nice, very nice." He rubbed his palms together nervously. "Karim!" he commanded in his high-pitched voice, "table for two." He turned to his customers. "Vindaloo very good tonight. Oh yes. Vindaloo I am recommending."

They sat down. On the pink tablecloth stood a cheap vase containing a posy of sad-looking artificial orchids. Willie pushed this aside, centred the glass ashtray and lit up. He ordered drinks, white wine for Gill, a pint for himself.

"I thought alcohol was against their religion," Gill observed.

"It is, but can you imagine pulling in Scottish punters if you didn't sell booze?"

"No, I can not."

They were handed menus.

"Matter of fact, Mo has a running battle with his folks here on the subject. Mo likes a drink."

"The proprietor is Mo's father?"

"Right. See, they don't mind corrupting infidels like us, if we insist on it, but they themselves are abstainers. And keen on keeping up the customs from the old country."

"But Mo doesn't go along with that?"

"He's a different generation. Born and educated here. Sometimes I think he's more patriotic than the majority of Scots!"

Gill nodded. "I can believe that. Has he rejected his religion then?"

"I think he goes with his Dad to the Mosque once or twice a year. Just to please him, you know. But really he's a lapsed sinner like me. He's a bit of a poet too. He's into Haiku. You know, minimalist stuff, originally Japanese."

Karim reappeared and they ordered chicken tikkas and two vindaloos.

"You mean ... I presume you were brought up a Catholic, Willie?"

He laughed. "You one of the Prods who can tell an RC at fifty paces?"

"Don't be daft," said Gill, picking up her glass.

"Oh yes, I was a good wee Papist as a laddie. First Communion, First Confession – the whole bit. And through the Catholic school system at St Columba's till I quit at sixteen. By that time I'd given away the faith completely."

"What happened?"

"What happened? Well, I saw how divisive the influence of the churches was in Scotland. Not as bad as Ireland, but basically the same." He supped from his pint. "And anyway, I just couldn't believe in the Christian claim to exclusivity, to having all the answers. Never mind the Virgin Birth, our eventual bodily resurrection etcetera. All that supernatural baloney."

"Some of it is hard to take in the modern age."

"Mind you, Gill, I'm not saying religious organizations don't do a huge amount of good as well. But in my opinion all that effort would be better secularized."

Gill put her head on one side. "Old folks and the very sick need the solace of religious beliefs though, Willie."

"I know. That's fine. What I'm talking about is the priests and ministers sticking their noses into fundamentally political issues. They're not trained for that. They only confuse sections of the population."

"You mean they should stick to the spiritual realm, I take it? But, Willie, what about South America? Some of those Catholic priests have shown unbelievable courage in pushing for social change."

"You're a bonny fechter, Gill! OK, circumstances alter cases. But, mind you, a lot of the misery in those places was actually originally *created* by the Church's armies when they arrogantly destroyed perfectly viable native polities."

"Native whats?"

"Polities. Social and governmental systems, which in those cases worked in long-standing harmony with their own religions."

The tikkas arrived, their spicy aroma delicious.

This man has brains and breadth of vision, thought Gill. "Come on, Willie. Off our high horses! Let's eat. These smell marvellous."

Later over lychees and then coffee, she told him something of herself.

"Pretty conventional, me. Born 1971, Bearsden. Educated Miss Patterson-White's kindergarten, Park School and Glasgow University. MA degree and Teacher's Certificate from Jordanhill. Father stockbroker, mother an artist. Hobbies, reading and listening to music, used to play hockey and still play tennis quite competently in the summer. Ambitions – rather vague, I'm afraid. To have fun, keep fit, spark off a little curiosity in the minds of some of the kids I teach. Oh ... and a family of my own one of these fine days."

"Uh-huh," was Willie's response.

"Boring, eh?"

"Not at all. Different though." He reached over the table, lifted her hand and kissed it briefly. "You're too modest, Gill. There's a lot more in that pretty head of yours than you let on. And I'm going to find out the real *you*. See if I don't!"

Just before he saw her on to a bus home, Willie put his arms around her and kissed her on the lips. Nothing was said. Just a gentle kiss.

Their meetings were now almost daily, if of varying duration, depending on each other's commitments. Gill soon came to feel that her day was incomplete without at least half an hour in Willie's company. Invariably some topic would come up on which he had a trenchant view to express, or he'd say something which made her laugh. She was learning such a lot from him. And she knew very well that Willie Devine was just as keen to see her whenever possible. She had a sense that he valued her opinions more than he made obvious.

Before long the restrictions of pubs, restaurants, parks became irksome.

"Listen, I'm knackered tonight, Gill. Would you come to my palatial residence for a cuppa?"

She nodded. Not long after, she was sitting on his lap in the small flat at Rubyvale Street while the kettle boiled. It was the first time they had been truly alone. They kissed, lightly at first, then fiercely. Soon they were entwined on the armchair their bodies pressed passionately together. A great mutual heat was generated. The whistling-kettle whistled and they drew apart.

"Yeow!" said Willie with a grin. "Intermission time."

They drank tea for a few moments but were soon in one another's arms again, this time on the carpet in front of the hissing gas fire. Willie's hand stole under Gill's jumper and inside her brassière. They were panting.

She took his wrist and firmly withdrew his hand. "Steady now, Willie. I'm not ready for that yet."

He sat upright on the floor. "Sorry, wee one. Nearly got carried away. Put it down to the Lapsang Souchong."

The unexpectedness of the remark had Gill giggling. The tense moment was defused and they laughed together, but as they looked into one another's eyes both knew it couldn't be long before they were lovers.

A week or two later, on a rainy Saturday afternoon with a silenced lurid Hindu film flickering meaninglessly on the TV set, they got into Willie's bed and devoured one another without restraint. Gill was not a virgin. Her first time had been after a rather liquid disco party, back in a final year medical student's room. Just after that he'd vanished to a hospital in Aberdeen. Then there'd been Charles, a young vet. He'd taken her out a few times and they'd gone in for some rather awkward experiments in the back of his car.

But nothing had prepared her for Willie's no-holds-barred, gloriously uninhibited and prolonged love making. He had to stifle her loud involuntary squeals as she experienced ever rising plateaux of orgasms. Lunging desperately to his own climax, he nevertheless managed to smile at her and say, "Wheesht, lassie! You'll disturb Mrs Skelly's nap downstairs."

It was wonderful. That evening she felt profoundly at peace, yet full of underlying energy too. Willie had to go into the office and so they parted early.

"Oh, Willie, thanks for everything. I ..."

He laid a finger on her lips. "Don't say anything, Gill. Let's not break the spell." He smiled and her heart melted. "Here's your bus. Till tomorrow." They kissed tenderly, not caring who saw.

Gill had so far forborne to tell her parents much about Willie. She was well aware that he would not at all fit into any of their preconceived notions of a suitable friend for their second daughter. Their first, Fiona, was safely married to a successful architect in Toronto, and they expected some comfortable arrangement along those lines in due course for Gill. Too bad. She was going to put them in the picture, for better or worse.

Tonight.

## TWO

THE REACTION WAS all too predictable.

"This young man doesn't sound our type at all. Quite frankly, Gill."

"He's not so young, Mum."

"Oh? What age is he then?"

"Thirty five."

"In that case he sounds even less suitable."

Gill sighed. She looked at her father.

"Where does he live?" he enquired neutrally.

"Partick."

"Oh my God! Partick?" Muriel MacIntyre looked disgusted.

"There are some parts that are not too bad. Round by ...," her husband began.

"Och, Bob, for heaven's sake! *Partick*."

"It's perfectly reasonable there, Mum, but actually I don't really care anyway. I consider it much more important what he does in life and what sort of a person he is than where he lives."

"Don't be deliberately naïve, Gill. In any case, didn't you say he works on the *Recorder*?"

"That's right."

"It's nothing but a damned rag for the working class. Royal sex scandals, sports. I wouldn't give it house room."

Gill sighed again. "When did you last read the paper, Mum?"

"I told you. I wouldn't have it in the house."

"Willie has his own column, under his own name, twice a week. I've read it and what he says is thoroughly worthwhile."

Robert tried again. "We have the *Recorder* on the table at the Western Club. I look at it occasionally. What did you say his surname was, Gill?"

Muriel cut in, changing tack. "Where was he educated?"

"The answer to your question, Dad, is Devine. And to yours, Mum, St Columba's in Partick."

"So he's RC, is he?"

"Well, by upbringing. But he doesn't have any time for it now."

"Oh yes, I'll believe that," snorted Muriel. "Once a Catholic, always ..."

"OK, Mum. OK. I know the line. Let's drop the subject, shall we? I'll not burden you with any more information about Willie."

"Just bear in mind our attitude, Gill." Muriel's face had coloured slightly with irritation.

"*My* attitude doesn't count, huh?"

"Now look here, young lady! Just you ..."

"Muriel, calm down," said Robert. "Gill is twenty four and quite level-headed, I'm sure." He turned to his daughter. "Listen, darling, why don't you bring Willie out to see us some time?"

"Bob!" Muriel was furious at her ever reasonable husband.

Gill smiled faintly at him. "I'll think about it, Dad. Thanks."

Further argument was headed off by a ring on the front door chimes.

"I'll get it," said Muriel, glad to leave the room.

"She'll cool off, Gill," said Robert quietly.

"I don't know, Dad. Anyway, she won't change anything, I can assure you of that."

There was a surprised shout in the hall, followed by shuffling feet. The sitting room door was flung open.

"Look who's here?" exclaimed Muriel, beaming. "James Ballantyne."

"Jamie!" Gill jumped up. "It's *years*!" She gave him a friendly kiss on the cheek.

"Good to see you all again," said Jamie. "Gill, Mr MacIntyre." He held out his hand to the older man.

"Come in, come in, Jamie! Sit down. This calls for a drink." Robert was delighted to be out of the firing line. "What'll it be?"

"Have you a dry sherry open?"

"Yes, of course. Same all round? Right. Won't be a jiffy."

The young man sat down.

"You're looking so well, Jamie," said Muriel. "And prosperous?"

"Can't complain, Mrs MacIntyre."

"Are you on a visit again, Jamie?" asked Gill. "You used to be up quite often. But of course your mum moved south."

"No. Actually I'm moving back to Glasgow. Just got in this afternoon."

He explained that he was temporarily living at the Automobile Club but would be looking to buy a flat, that he'd been promoted by his advertising company, Mekay & Schwartz, and sent to open a new Scottish office for them in Glasgow. There were congratulations all round and then reminiscing about childhood days.

Jamie knew his manners and didn't stay long, saying he wanted to get his papers in order for an early start in the morning. Gill saw him out. At the door he gave her a valedictory peck on the cheek, then said, "It's great to see you again, Gill. Really. I've often thought about you, in my various places of exile."

"The wee girl next door?"

"Something like that. Could we meet, d'you think? It would be nice to chat. We were good friends once, weren't we, Gill?"

"Yes, we were, Jamie. Actually I do have a friend who ..."

Jamie held up a hand. "Look, I didn't expect you'd be uninvolved. A star turn like you! All I'm suggesting we do is have tea in Princes' Square or something wild like that! For old time's sake, Gill." He took out his car keys. "Or a spin up Loch Lomond in that monster if you prefer." He pointed out to the Mercedes, parked under a street light in Muirlaw Drive.

Gill patted him on the arm. "You're obviously doing well, Jamie. Brilliant. I'm so pleased."

"May I give you a ring then, when I've found my feet?"

"Yes, OK, Jamie. Why not?"

As she closed the door she told herself that even if Willie Devine did completely fill her horizons, she should try to maintain other friendships, male as well as female. After all, she wasn't married to Willie or even engaged. Not yet, anyway.


Willie was informed about the reaction at Bearsden.

"It's my mother. She's so damned conservative, with a big and a small 'c'. Dad's fine. I'm not saying you'd agree politically. I mean, as a stockbroker he can hardly be expected to sing 'The Red Flag' for his party piece, can he?"

"Meaning?"

"Meaning? Well, Willie, I ... well ..."

"I don't have any party pieces which I perform, Comrade Gill."

"That's a vintage Devine enigmaticism!"

"Ah well, let it so remain." He grinned. "I take it then that the projected pilgrimage is off?" He turned down the corners of his mouth. "Dearie me. Whitna peety."

"You won't get off as easily as that. Give me another week or two, Willie. I *want* them to meet you."

A few evenings later Muriel was out visiting her friend Janey Smith. Gill took the opportunity to lobby her father.

"Dad, we got at cross purposes the other day about my friend Willie Devine."

"Yes, well, you know your mother. She's awfully choosy about people's backgrounds and all that."

"You mean she's a snob."

Robert rotated an open-fingered hand back and forth noncommittally. "I wouldn't put it as baldly as that. Remember she's artistic. Tends to see things, outside her painting and sculpture anyway, in black and white terms. A woman of considerable standards, Gill, your Mum."

"I know. And she's quite entitled to her views, even if most of them are out of date in my opinion. But she's *not* entitled to abuse and dismiss everyone who doesn't happen to belong to her social circle and share her outlook."

"No. Of course I agree with that, in principle at least, Gill, my dear."

She smiled at her father. What a thoroughly nice man he was. "Well, look, Dad. Willie is my very good friend and I really do want my parents to know him too. Could you speak to Mum, d'you think? Get her to agree that I bring him out one day?"

"Say no more. I'll give you the word when the groundwork's been done." He winked.

It was in fact about six days before Gill received the signal. Straight away she spoke to Willie and a visit was planned for the following Sunday afternoon.

In the meantime someone else called at Muirlaw Drive. Major Hector Colquhoun parked his landrover and walked briskly over to his daughter's house.

"Daddy! Come in. It's raw out there."

"Oh it's fresh, Muriel." He kissed her. "I've been into town on a few errands. Was passing and thought I'd like a drop of your China tea, if you don't mind."

"Mind? Don't be silly. You know I always love to see you. Heavens! You're only, well, less than an hour up there by Fintry, but we don't meet nearly often enough."

"True, but you have your lives and I mine. Tell me, how's Bob and the dear Gill? Any news from Canada?"

"Fiona's all right in Toronto, I think. Bob's as ever. Gill – well, to be frank, Daddy, I'm a little anxious."

"Oh?" The Major's weatherbeaten brow creased.

"Yes, she appears to have got in tow with some journalist."

"Ah, I see." The creases left his brow. "Romance. When that element enters the picture, Muriel, cool reason can fly out of the window."

"Yes. If it was a passing fancy – you know, a sort of delayed 'lorry driver phase', I wouldn't worry. But this sounds stupidly serious."

He followed her into the kitchen where she put the kettle on and opened a Tupperware box of homemade almond biscuits.

"My favourites," he said, touching her hand in gratitude. Then he enquired, "You say this chap's a journalist?"

"On the *Glasgow Recorder*."

"Mmm. Don't see it often. What's his line? Soccer? Pederastic priests?"

"Unfortunately not. Politics. I gather he has his own bi-weekly column."

"Does he, by Jove? Must be bright. I'd jolly well like to meet him. In my view the whole place is going to pot. Scotland, I mean. In some ways anyway. I wonder what he thinks. What's his name?"

"Willie Devine."

"You know I believe I've heard of him, Muriel."

"If you listen to Gill, we must be about the only people in the country whose tongues are not *hanging out* for his every statement."

Major Colquhoun's eyebrows lifted. "Is that so?"

They drank tea.

Muriel put down her teacup and saucer on the solid pine kitchen table. "If you really want to meet this individual, Daddy, he'll be here next Sunday afternoon. With any luck the visit won't recur."

"I might drop in." He laid a hand on his daughter's fine wool-clad shoulder. "Mr Devine sounds a bit out of our normal run, Muriel, but Gill wouldn't like him unless he were worthwhile. I'm sure of that."

"Maybe so, but he's obviously from the lowest of the low. Some slum, I wouldn't be surprised. Just because he's clawed his way up in a rag of a newspaper doesn't change that."

"Oh, I think these days we must give folks a chance, Muriel. I'm 75 but even I recognise that the old social system's dead and buried. And no bad thing."

"It's all right for you, Daddy."

He nodded understandingly. "D'you know, one of the chaps I was shooting with last week turned out to be a damned bookmaker!" He laughed, but there was no reaction from Muriel. "Look here, my dear, I expect this fellow's quite prickly. Background like that plus brains. Bound to make him sensitive. I knew quite a lot like that in the Regiment. But as long as they were shown a bit of, what shall I say? ... firm-handed kindness, if you know what I mean, they were all right. I had no difficulty getting on with them. Liked them very much, as a matter of fact. Wonderful in the Western Desert they were. Salt of the earth, the Jocks."

"Well?"

"I think it may pay to be somewhat diplomatic. You know, try not to provoke a row or anything like that. I'm thinking of Gill. If she's keen on the fellow she'd be bound to stand up for him. I'd hate to think of a breach. She's a darling lassie."

Muriel looked round directly at the Major, who was frowning. "I'll do my best, Daddy."


Gill took a phone call in the staffroom.

"Gill? Hi! It's me, Jamie."

"Oh, hello, Jamie. How's it going?"

"Great. I've found office premises which will do a treat and I think I've got a flat lined up."

"Well done. You certainly get a move on, Jamie."

He chortled confidently. "Listen, I'm going over to see the flat this afternoon. It's off Byres Road. That's not far from you is it?"

"No, just up the road."

"Would you come with me? Second opinion? I could pick you up from the school. When are you free?"

Gill was interested in other people's accommodation. One day she'd get a place of her own. Her curiosity was aroused. "OK, Jamie. I'd like that. I'm out at about four thirty."

"Right. That's great Gill. I'll be waiting for you. *Au revoir*!"

The Mercedes looked like a large exotic fish unexpectedly beached on a dreary debris-strewn shore. As she slid into its luxurious brushed nylon interior Gill was aware of many eyes upon them. She had to admit to herself that it was a relief when they slid away from Partick and turned north to the West End's douce terraces and crescents.

The top-floor flat in total was small, with one bedroom only, but the living area was disproportionately large, having served as a billiards room in more spacious mansioned days. Its glass roof gave the whole place an unusual airy ambience. The little kitchenette had been neatly modernized. Gill was charmed. Jamie signed a provisional lease there and then and took two sets of keys from Miss Hetherington, the estate agent's representative. They left.

"This calls for a celebration!" said Jamie, thoroughly pleased with the transaction. "Where shall we go? I'm a bit out of date in that department."

Internally Gill squirmed. Her instinct was to take Jamie somewhere neutral, *anywhere* Willie was sure not to be. But she was not a coward. She'd already told Jamie she had a special boyfriend. Before she could think better of it she said, "There's a pub near my school where I often go with some others. My friend's usually there at this hour."

Jamie put a thumb in the air. "Great. Let's go." He made to get into the car.

Gill shook her head. "I think you should leave it here, Jamie. Safer than Partick."

"Oh, right. We walk then?"

"It isn't far."

"This all sounds very intriguing. Good for the soul to hobnob with the hoi polloi now and then. Yes? Tell me about your friend. What does he do for a crust?"

Gill told Jamie briefly about Willie. They entered the Argyle.

"Wow! Certainly a proletarian watering-hole, Gill. You come here *often*?"

"Oh yes, Jamie." She smiled.

"Guid auld Glesca, I suppose," he responded without much enthusiasm.

"Hullo, Gill! How're y'daein?"

"Lex! I'm fine thanks. This is Jamie Ballantyne, an old friend."

Lex Grant nodded expressionlessly. "Uh-huh," he mumbled. "I'm on my way tae the toilet."

Willie was in his corner. He waved them over. Jamie was introduced. Beside Mo Hossein sat a small morose-looking man in a workman's donkey-jacket.

"This is Tommy Bell. An old drinking pal of mine. We go back for yonks. That right, Tommy?"

"Aye, right enough, Willie," was the deadpan reply.

They sat down. Lex returned.

Jamie was not going to be put off his stride.

"I gather you're with the *Recorder*, Willie."

"Yes. What about yourself?"

"Advertising game. I'm with an American outfit. We're opening in Glasgow. I've just come back."

"Back from where?"

"London. Mainly there, although I did a training stint in New York."

"Oh aye."

There was a slight awkwardness. Mo took orders and went up to the bar.

Gill asked the newcomer: "Tommy, are you at the *Recorder* too?"

"No," he replied unhelpfully.

"Tommy's a scribbler like me, but not journalism. Novels. Stories."

"Really?" said Jamie. "I always wanted to write. Never found the time. What are your subjects? Thrillers, sagas?"

Tommy Bell lifted his head, as it seemed, wearily. "Sex. Poverty. The abysmal state of Scotland. Suchlike."

Jamie's mouth fell open.

"Tommy's gaun places, I'm tellin' ye," remarked Lex.

For the first time that Gill could recall Mo spoke up: "His writing's very good. Like poetry sometimes, so it is."

"Have you published much, Tommy?" Gill enquired.

"Two novels and a collection of short stories," was the tired, half-shut-eyed reply. "And pamphlets."

Thoughtful sipping and deep draught taking ensued all round.

Jamie was accustomed to keeping up his conversational end. "Have you worked in the South, Willie? The *Recorder*'s part of the Amalgamated Press Group, isn't it?"

"Never seen the need myself."

"Perhaps not. I just think it's a good thing to get experience in the big world out there. Widen one's horizons and all that."

"There's more than enough for Scots to do in Scotland. Those with real ties here."

"I agree wi' that, Willie," said Lex. "Nae need t'gae gallivantin' aroon the globe."

Jamie had turned a little pale. Gill was beginning to feel uncomfortable. This had been a risk. She'd better say something quickly.

"I suppose a lot depends on the nature of the job, Willie. If you're with an international firm you're bound to be sent to different places."

He was not to be deflected. "You have the choice, Gill, whether to join such a company or not."

Jamie decided it was not worth being drawn further into an argument. "I'm not at all sure we make that kind of choice deliberately. One goes where opportunity offers, No? Well, that's been my motto anyway. And it doesn't seem to have done me any harm so far." He laughed in comradely fashion.

"That depends," said Lex heavily.

Jamie shrugged. "All I can say is I thoroughly enjoyed my time in the States, and London is great fun too. I suppose nowadays I'd call myself a cosmopolitan."

Lex grunted. "That's the trouble with people like you. Fuckin' cosmopolitans."

Jamie now reddened. "I resent that remark."

"Is that right, son?" said Lex patronizingly. "Well, for your information, we here are not fuckin' cosmopolitans. We're *Nationalists*!"

"Yes, but look, I'm just as ..."

Gill glanced at her watch. She had to stop this. Willie was staring at the ceiling. "I have to go, Jamie?"

"Oh. OK. Yes, I'll come with you."

"See you tomorrow perhaps," she said to the other four, waving. She'd sort this out with Willie as soon as possible.

They walked up to Jamie's car. He offered to drive her home and she accepted.

"That lot can be a bit parochial, Jamie."

"I'll say."

"Hope you weren't offended?"

Jamie expelled air through his teeth in a mildly disgusted gesture. "No, not really. Your Willie's a character. I can see that. But the others – well, I'm afraid I'll not be rushing to chat them up again."

"Lex is a poet, you know. He was on TV recently. Mo writes too. I hadn't met Tommy Bell before."

"Amazing. But then writers are notoriously not very nice people. All complexes and jealousies. No doubt the Scottish variety is no different."

"That's rather sweeping, Jamie."

"Oh well." The Mercedes purred its way through Milngavie. "What does Willie Devine actually write about in the *Recorder*?"

"Topical issues with a political angle. Mainly with specific reference to Scottish affairs."

"You mean Devolution, Home Rule, Independence? All that crap?"

"Those are the subjects most often in the column, Jamie. I'm afraid I don't accept your description though."

"Are you a Scot Nat then, Gill?"

"I haven't made up my mind fully."

Jamie could see his tenuous friendship with this damnably attractive girl slipping away, maybe irretrievably.

"You always were a girl with a mind of her own, Gill. I admire that." He reached over and squeezed her hand, smiling. "Of course, I've been away for quite a while. Things change. I'd really like to have a good chinwag with Willie some time. Get up to date." A motorbike overtook them from the inside lane, swerving across their front, uncomfortably close. Jamie snorted, lowered his window and screamed out, "*Arsehole*!" Shutting the window, he apologized, "Pardon my French."

Gill looked at him briefly. Jamie Ballantyne had certainly grown up. His profile was clean-cut, decidedly manly. He was a handsome specimen. His hands on the wheel were pale-skinned, strong. He radiated youthful energy.

"I'll make sure you and Willie meet again," she said, almost to herself.

They parted, Gill having agreed that Jamie might ring her again, but not for perhaps a week or two. He said this suited him since he was going to be in orbit outfitting the new office and his flat. Then he put his arm round her, cradled her chin in his cupped hand and kissed her full on the lips.

Her mind in a state of mild, not unpleasant confusion, Gill closed the front door and met her father in the hall.

"Hello, Dad. Jamie Ballantyne gave me a lift home."

"That was handy. How did you meet?"

"Let me get my coat off and I'll tell you."

"Right. Your mother and I are just about to have a pre-supper sherry. Join us?"

"Lovely, Dad. With you in a minute."

She explained Jamie's quick progress and described the flat he'd taken.

"He always was a go-ahead young fellow," remarked Muriel approvingly.

"We went for a drink after. I introduced him to Willie and some of his friends."

"Really?" Muriel's tone indicated that she was uninterested in pursuing the matter.

"Yes. Quite funny, in a way," Gill persisted.

Robert smiled. "An unusual conversational cocktail?"

"Not to say a Molotov cocktail, Dad!"

"I should think a young man of initiative like Jamie would have been rather bored. I mean, he's been around. Travelled a good deal abroad. What did you find to talk about?" Muriel's eyebrows stayed elevated awaiting a reply.

Robert poured small top-ups, taking his time and emitting small phatic grunts. He'd had a busy day and did not want to have to suffer the shrill exchanges of another mother and daughter fight. To no avail.

"We spoke about literature. A chap called Tommy Bell was there. He's had novels and short stories published."

"Never heard of him." Muriel's eyebrows returned to their normal position.

"No, well neither have I actually. I expect it takes time for a writer's name to be known."

"What does he write about, Gill?" asked Robert.

"Difficult to be sure, not having read anything of his, but I gather he deals mainly with the contemporary scene in Scotland."

"I suppose a man like Willie Devine is bound to attract writers, media people. An interesting group, I should think."

"Yes, they are, Dad. Unconventional backgrounds, some of them, and maybe different life-styles too, but I think they're talented."

Muriel finished her sherry. "Just as long as their talents are usefully employed. Dare one say, *artistically* employed?"

Gill felt a suppressed irritation struggling for release. "I take it, Mum, you'd admit poetry as 'artistic'? Several of the group are poets."

"That entirely depends on what they write. Most of the so-called poetry being churned out today I wouldn't waste my time looking at. Meaningless, whining, self-indulgent doggerel."

"I see."

"Oh, come on, Gill! Don't pretend you approve of that tripe. We've both laughed before now at some of the examples in your English course. Brodsky, Peter Porter. You remember? Incomprehensible rubbish."

Quietly Gill acquiesced. "I remember. Yes. It's just that I haven't yet had a chance to read any of their work. Lex Grant's been on TV."

"Has he?" said Robert, nodding pleasantly.

Muriel stood up. "That's no guarantee of *anything*. Not nowadays."

Suddenly Gill was angry. Why should she put up with her mother's negativism? She blurted out, "I do hope you're not going to pour cold water on *everything* when Willie's here on Sunday, Mum?"

"I shall behave in a civilized manner and expect your friend to do the same," she replied icily.

Once again Robert headed off further argument. "We're looking forward to meeting Willie, Gill. He sounds a most unusual chap, and pretty damned clever too. I'm sure we'll get on fine." He rose. "That casserole smells great, Muriel. Can I set the kitchen table for you?"

The meal was indeed delicious and tensions relaxed. Muriel told them of a new commission she'd received.

"Janey Smith wants a selection of pen and ink sketches for her gift-shop. Local scenes round about Milngavie and Bearsden. She's asked me to do them. I'm quite excited."

Congratulations were duly offered.

"Is there a deadline?"

"October thirty-first Bob. Janey's going to have packets of notelets made up in time to catch the Christmas trade."

"Well done again," came the loyal response from her husband.

Gill took her coffee up to bed with her. Despite the comfort of good food she felt a nagging peripheral nervousness. Dully she knew that her mother and Willie would not tolerate one another. Had she ever supposed so? Crazy. But if there was to be an explosion where would that leave her? Willie had no skill in parrying near-insults, or at least, more accurately, he was unlikely to be willing to deploy the necessary patience to keep the peace. He'd speak his mind: Muriel MacIntyre was sure to do the same.

It was several hours before Gill sank into a troubled sleep.

## THREE

SUNDAY CAME. During lunch it started to rain and by three thirty there was a downpour. Willie stood drenched on the doorstep at Muirlaw Drive. He had neither a cap nor umbrella and so his black hair was wetly plastered to his head. His trouser bottoms and old blue anorak were soaked.

Gill ushered him into the small bathroom off the hall and handed him a towel. "Here, dry yourself off, Willie. Have you a comb?"

"Don't carry one."

She fetched one for him. They entered the sitting room.

"Mum, Dad, this is a rather damp Willie Devine!"

Muriel smiled primly. Robert got up and tentatively offered his hand but the other man did not seem to know quite how to respond. Immediately an atmosphere of embarrassment invaded the room.

Gill felt herself flushing. She fussed to cover the moment. "Poor man. What a day! Here, Willie, sit here near the radiator."

"You know, Muriel," said Robert, "I believe some tea right now wouldn't go amiss. What about you, Willie?" He winked encouragingly.

"Aye, right enough. A warmer, eh?"

"That's it."

Muriel left wordlessly and was soon back, wheeling a noiseless trolley, silver tea-set and china on the top shelf, cakes and biscuits below. Tea was poured and side-plates handed out.

"Gill's shown us some of your recent pieces in the *Recorder*, Willie. How long have you had your own column?" Robert was determined to be hospitable.

"It's a couple of years now. I was lucky. Harry Smart died suddenly. Heart attack. That's how I got my chance."

"Ah," said Robert, "I think I recall that. He was pretty well known, wasn't he?"

"He did some good work in his day, yes."

Gill joined in at last. "I'm sorry about Mr Smart, but the paper must have been glad to be able to promote you, Willie."

"Oh well, I've not had too many complaints. Bar maybe I'm not attentive enough to possible libel risks. Hammering the Government, naming names and all that." He grinned, slightly.

Muriel poured second cups of tea. The rain intensified, pinging on the window panes. "Would you just listen to that?" she said.

"Bloody monsoon," Willie replied.

Robert cleared his throat and laughed lightly. "At least you can't blame Westminster for the weather, Willie."

There was no echoing laugh.

"I blame them for Scotland's abysmal housing stock, half of it full of damp, ruining people's health."

Muriel finally had to speak. "It's those Labour-run Local Councils that are at fault. Inefficient and corrupt to a man. Or woman."

Willie put down his cup and saucer. "Governments, local or otherwise, are all inefficient, Mrs MacIntyre. But Scotland's housing situation is a scandal. Not round here of course."

"Quite," said Muriel, "But I still say those awful councils are at the root of it. All the wrong spending priorities."

Gill made her contribution. "There's something in that, Mum, I agree. Lovely fraternal trips overseas for the boys etcetera. But if there's inadequate funding in the first place it wouldn't much help reining in on a few freebies. Some of my kids live in rotten conditions. It's not right in 1995."

"Mind you," said Robert, "Things are very much better than they were when I was a boy. A lot's been done, but you can only go as far as the national purse will stretch at any one time. An immutable principle of business, however frustrating, Willie."

"There's no cash shortage, Mr MacIntyre."

"Well, what I had in mind was the recent economic recession. The consequent cut in tax revenues."

Muriel leaned back in her comfortable padded chair. The suite was covered in pleasing brick and cream willow-pattern fabric. "And there's the seemingly bottomless pit of the Health Service, the cost of keeping up our nuclear deterrent. I think the Government works wonders, frankly."

Gill had a good idea what was coming. Willie faced her parents.

"See, that's the trouble with some folks. They can't, or won't, face the real position. Westminster control is for them a fixture, the source of everything. The truth is it's the opposite. Take, take, take. By now Scotland's just about completely sapped. What's needed is..."

Muriel said loudly, "Rubbish! We receive more per head of Government handouts than the English people themselves. Everybody knows that."

Robert backed her up. "You'd have to accept that now, Willie?"

He shook his head vigorously. "No, I would not."

"Can you explain, Willie?" asked Gill.

"It's a long story and statistics are elusive, Gill."

"Maybe," said Muriel, "But one can't just go around making statements like that without being able to support them."

Willie looked at her levelly. "I'm quite able to justify what I say, Mrs MacIntyre. The time just didn't seem right to go into the subject." He spoke quietly. "However, for your information, the round figures for public expenditure per capita in recent years have been about £4,000 in Scotland and £3,500 in England. But ..."

"There you are then," said Muriel, pleased.

"I was going on to qualify that," Willie retorted, rather more sharply now. "Those numbers refer only to *easily identifiable* projects like hospitals, all the public services, and roads. Roads especially, Scotland being so empty and relatively inaccessible. But there's huge additional expenditure in England – things subsidies to Defence contractors, mostly in South East England, mortgage tax relief and so on – none of that's computed in the same way. Anyway, because of the state of things here Scots have again been emigrating steadily for two decades. The population's been falling as a result, which further distorts the real statistics."

Silence greeted this speech. Gill regarded Willie with a look compounded of curiosity and respect. Robert nodded slowly as he digested the information. Muriel frowned. She was an intelligent woman, resilient. "So, what's your solution? Insist on even more subsidies from Westminster, I suppose?"

Willie smiled. "Och, listen, we'll be here all day if you get me on my soap-box."

Muriel was not to be put off. "No, tell us. Are you going to campaign in that paper of yours for even more cash for your friends in those dreadful left-wing councils? *Unearned* money for them to squander on hare-brained schemes? So-called 'Gay Support Groups'? That sort of ridiculous thing?"

Willie had stopped smiling. "I do not have any particular friends on councils. But I'm sure most of those public servants do a good job." He reached into his pocket, then hesitated. "D'you mind if I smoke?"

Gill intervened. "We don't do it in the house, Willie." She tried to make light of the matter. "If you're desperate we could go and stand in the conservatory at the door. Can't go outside in the rain."

"Never mind," he muttered.

Muriel ignored the interruption. "I don't agree. Most of your 'public servants' are actually public enemies, leeches, or worse. They're nearly all Socialists of one colour or another, or irresponsible Nationalists, or Catholics. What can you expect? All pulling in different directions. And with extremely dubious loyalties." She pursed her lips, then spat out, "Rotten traitors, the lot of them, I've no doubt!"

Willie was finally stung to anger. "Och, that's just prejudice. You can't tell all Catholics, Socialists and Nationalists to belt up. Just to go back into their holes and die. Even the English so-called Constitution's supposed to guarantee fuckin' free speech, isn't it?"

Muriel looked at the ceiling of her recently redecorated sitting room. "I really would appreciate it if you'd try to avoid obscenities..."

The arid exchanges went on a bit longer. But it was clear that the visit was a failure. Compromises were not on the menu. Battle lines were drawn. Eventually Willie stood up waving his hands dismissively.

"I'm not sitting here listening to this any longer, Gill."

She was thoroughly unhappy. "I'll see you to the bus, Willie. I'm sorry ... I ..."

Her mother barked a stiff, "Right," and left the room, her husband in tow. Robert threw over his shoulder, "Take my golf umbrella, Gill."

When she returned to the house her grandfather's landrover was outside.

"Gill, my dear," said Major Colquhoun, kissing her affectionately on the cheek. "I'm sorry to have missed your Willie. Caused quite a stir, I gather?"

"You could say that, Grandpa."

"So grim?"

Suddenly Gill was overcome by a combination of surging anger and debilitating despair. Tears threatened. "There's no point talking about it. No doubt Mum will tell you all. Her version of course."

"Oh dear," said the Major.

Gill couldn't stay with them. "Please excuse me, Grandpa. I've some work upstairs. For tomorrow's classes. I'd better ..."

He put his arm round her shoulders. "I quite understand, darling. Off you go."

As she stumbled upstairs her tears began to fall. She threw herself on the bed and, for a while, sobbed uncertainly into her pillow. It was convenient at home, she loved her parents, at least, she and her mother had always been able to tolerate one another, and her father was a dear. Friends often called. All her books were here. She looked round the room at many totems of her childhood. "Oh, God," she groaned. But the bitterly opposed attitudes that had surfaced that afternoon would never be reconciled. And Gill decided now that she wanted keenly to break with her mother's inflexible conservatism.

Perhaps an hour later she lifted the phone extension beside her bed and dialled a number noted in her diary.

"Cathie? It's Gill. Is that second room of yours still free?"

"Yes. Why?"

"Could I have it?"

"Sure, Gill. That'd be great. I need the money and I'm sure we'd get on. When were you thinking of?"

"Tonight. If that's all right."

"Well! Yes, I don't mind but, Gill, what's happened?"

Gill swallowed. "Just say I suddenly got tired of being a homebird."

"All right, Gill."

"I'll be over in say a couple of hours, Cathie. And thanks."

"No problem. Spag Bol OK?"

"Brilliant."

Gill felt much better. Briskly she began to pack a bag.


Muriel had made some fresh tea and Major Colquhoun sat in the sitting room enjoying it with a slice of madeira cake containing caraway seeds.

"So 'Oor Wullie' didn't appeal, Muriel?"

"Ugh, nothing more than a bolshie boor, Daddy."

"Bob? How did he strike you?"

Robert's head went on one side in a typical gesture. "Well, he's clearly a political animal. Not my favourite species or one I'm much familiar with."

"I should hope not, Bob! Not that type anyhow," said Muriel.

"I think you were a bit hard on him, dear. I mean you conceded nothing, lashing out at Catholics, Labour and the Scot Nats. To be honest, I wasn't surprised he blew up. Not that I'm disagreeing with you basically, of course. It's just ..."

The Major turned to look his daughter in the face. "Sounds to me as if you provoked him, Muriel. I'd hoped that wouldn't happen till we'd all got to know the man a bit." His face registered disapproval.

"That's not accurate at all!" Muriel slapped the arm of her chair smartly. "*He* provoked *me* ... with his squalid statistics. No doubt he could justify *anything*."

Robert sat upright. "I know what you mean, Muriel, in a way, but actually, Hector, he did seem to be on top of the figures. The comparative up-to-date government spending in England versus Scotland."

"Did he?" said the Major, interested.

"I for one gained the distinct impression that he could have produced a lot more specific facts about other areas if, say, he'd been under challenge on a platform or on a TV question programme."

Muriel said in some irritation, "You can make all the excuses you like, Bob. Did you see his shoes?"

"What? I beg your pardon?"

"His shoes. Or boots, I think they were. Hadn't seen a brush or polish since they were bought, I shouldn't wonder."

The Major laughed. "You always were good at taking evasive action, Muriel! Bit like your dear mother."

"Yes, well ..." she responded with a not very good grace.

The tea trolley was wheeled to the other side of the room.

"You know, I really am sorry I missed Willie."

"Daddy! Why do you *say* that?"

"Because I know the type, Muriel. Met them often enough in the Regiment. Fair supply of barrack-room lawyers in the H L I, I assure you! But some of the best characters often came in as bolshie as hell. Miserable backgrounds, hellish upbringing. But get them well fed and fit, show them some discipline and a bit of appreciation and – hey presto! you've got one of the best soldiers in the world. Salt of the earth, I used to say."

Muriel sighed. "Yes, I know. That's all very well as long as they're in clearly subordinate positions, not running the country."

Robert interjected, "That's a rather unwarranted jump, Muriel. All

Willie was talking about, if I understood him, was the need for additional funds from Central Government to tackle particular Scottish problems. Bad housing he mentioned. Dampness from our climate, which in turn leads to unnecessary demands on the Health Service. That sort of recognition of realities north of the Border."

Muriel sighed again. "You must have realized that he was hinting at a break with the Union, to give Labour total control here of course. So he and his ilk can call the shots without Westminster's moderating influence."

Unaccountably the Major laughed a second time. "My old father used to warn against 'the Cloth Cap Brigade getting on top'. He was a wise man. But, there again, fundamentally, folks in those days were really not democratic at all. Ah well ..." He dabbed his gingerish moustache in a gesture the others recognized as indicating that the active seventy five year old was about to depart. "I'd still like to meet Mr Willie Devine some time. I'll give Gill a ring. Oh, Muriel, say good-bye to my grand-daughter won't you? Thanks, dear. I want to get back to Fintry before the dark closes in. Filthy night."

About seven Gill came downstairs with a large suitcase, a rucksack and two voluminous plastic bags.

"Gill! What on earth ... ?"

"I'm moving out, Mum. Going to stay with Cathie Lonie. You know, she works with me at Rowley Street."

"But Gill ... why ... will you be all right? What shall we say?"

Robert appeared. He was distressed. "Darling! Don't go. Please. What can we ... ?"

"Please don't fuss, both of you." Gill felt quite collected.

"But why must you go, Gill?" Robert persisted. "Is it because of this afternoon?"

"Surely you're not going to let that Willie creature break up our family?" Muriel had very quickly got any emotion under control.

"That 'Willie creature', as you put it, is a dear friend of mine whom I admire very much." She deliberately turned her back on her mother. "It's a wrench to leave you, Dad, but I'm twenty four. It isn't so odd to want a bit of independence, is it?" She turned to Muriel. "That shouldn't be hard for you to sell to the neighbours."

There was no reply.

"If you insist on going, at least let me drive you, Gill."

"Well, I would appreciate that, Dad. It's just down to Jordanhill and it's still pouring. Here's Cathie's phone number and the address." She put on her raincoat and picked up the rucksack and plastic bags. Robert grabbed a short sheepskin jacket and lifted the suitcase. "I'll keep in touch and see you soon, I expect," said Gill without much conviction.

Suddenly whimpering Muriel said, "Oh God!" and fled into the kitchen.


All next day Gill experienced a feeling of unreality. For twenty four years she'd had a firm base at Muirlaw Drive: suddenly it had gone. Cathie had welcomed her and been kind enough, but Gill had slept badly in the unfamiliar bed. She longed for the evening and a chance to tell Willie what she'd done.

He was not in the Argyle. She sat with Lex and Mo. Cathie had accompanied her and, a bit later, Hamish MacCorquodale came in for a couple of pints.

"Hello now! It's Gill, is it not? Cathie? How d'you do, Cathie. Well, how goes it, ladies?"

"Fine, Hamish. You?"

"Chust great! I'm into a new series for the T V all about life in the Scottish Gaeltacht. From pre-history right through the Middle Ages – The Culdee Church and all that – The Lords of the Isles, the Jacobites, the Clearances and since. It's one hell of a story, I'm telling you and tragic, tragic ..." His large expressive face indicated an awful pain. "But the thread through it all is the language and how it has survived every attempt to suppress it."

"When'll the series be ready?" asked Lex.

"Towards the middle of next year maybe. Oh, I've great hopes of this programme, Lex," Hamish enthused. "Of course the Gaelic revival has been on the go now for a year or two with the group Runrig and other developments, but this could be a powerful dig in the ribs. Oh yes."

"Whose ribs?" Cathie enquired.

Hamish put back his head and gave vent to one of his explosive staccato laughs, momentarily freezing to incredulity the gesticulating Glasgow disputants at the bar.

"Whose ribs is it?" he eventually repeated, panting. "Well now, there's those bloody eedjits on the banks of the River Thames. Right, Lex?"

"Aye, right."

"Then there's the education authorities, with their standardized curricula and the rest of it. And the Scottish media bosses – them that's responsible for minorities' programme allocations anyway. There's the Gaels themselves too. They're the worst for chust letting their priceless cultural heritage slip away through their fingers, like... like the fine white grains of sand on a Hebridean beach."

By now the Highlander's moist brown eyes were on a far-off shore.

Mo Hossein offered a rare comment: "That's a most important point. The point about minorities' TV programmes. Most important indeed."

Hamish regarded him with dawning comprehension. He smiled charmingly and said, "Did you know we have Pakistani shopkeepers in Stornoway who can speak Gaelic?"

Time moved on but there was no sign of Willie. Gill asked Lex if he thought he'd come.

"Cannae tell, Gill girl. They journalists are a law tae theirsels. Prob'ly in some editorial pow-wow. Could be oors. Mebbe he won't show the night at a'."

Eventually she left with Cathie, miserable that she'd not seen Willie. She hid her feelings.

"What d'you think of Lex Grant, Cathie?"

"A fraud."

"What? What do you mean?"

"That aggressive Glesca accent. The limited vocab. It's an act."

"How d'you know, Cathie?"

"I've seen some of his poetry."

"Have you?"

"Yes, in 'little magazines'."

"But I thought he wrote in Scots."

"Right, Gill, he does. Although what constitutes authentic Scots in 1995 – search me. But it's not Glesca-speak, that's for sure. Anyhow, he also writes in English."

"So? What's it like, the English verse?"

"Well, not bad – if you like that sort of thing. Sans metre, sans rhyme, plenty of Anglo-Saxon taboo words, as the dictionaries put it, only occasional flashes of ambiguous meaning."

Gill laughed. "You're not a great fan of modern poetry I take it, Cathie?"

"With a few notable exceptions, an *aficionado* I am not, Gill."

Their bus arrived.

"So if that's not Lex's natural speech, why d'you think he does it?"

"Politics? Working class solidarity? Laziness? Inferiority complex?"

"O K. I get the idea." Gill laughed again.

"Maybe he thinks it's patriotic to emphasize a crushing provincialism. If so, he's a bigger fool than he looks."

"Let's change the subject," said Gill.

Willie was absent the following evening too. Gill rang his home number but got no reply. On the Wednesday she ran into him outside the school.

"Willie!" She kissed him quickly. "Where've you been?"

"Edinburgh. You'll have heard about the demos at the Scottish Assembly building?"

"Yes, I have, but what were you ... ?"

"Observing. The editor sent me through to get the flavour of things. Nice room in the Mount Royal. Nothing but the best."

"How was it? The demonstrations?"

Willie turned his right hand palm upwards. "Much the usual, really. A mixture of nutters, Celtic fringe maniacs, Greens, some professional hard men looking for a fight. But mainly decent, dead earnest folks doing their bit to raise the public's consciousness." They began walking towards the Argyle. "I knew a lot of people. Nationalists, a couple of MPs, a Glasgow lawyer I've used once or twice. Specialist in libel defence."

"Was there any violence?"

"The police were pretty rough. There was some blood. I believe three were taken to hospital. But nothing too serious." They reached the Argyle's entrance. Willie paused and said, "Not on this occasion anyway."

Gill was struck, not for the first time in their friendship, by the utter seriousness in his face.

They joined Lex, Mo and Tommy Bell, who had his wife with him. Quietly Gill told Willie of her move to Cathie Lonie's flat.

"I couldn't stay after last Sunday."

"Gill, I'm sorry," he said immediately. "I didn't mean to cause such a bloody row."

"It was my mother. She was impossible."

"Aye, well, I have to say she seemed out to get me all right. Is she always like that?"

Gill considered. "She's always had a temper and ... you know, strong views. But the last year or so she seems to have got more brittle, quite hostile really to anything or anybody that doesn't chime with her preconceived notions. It's Dad I pity."

"He seemed a reasonable bloke. A bit confused maybe."

"No, I think he knows quite well what he believes in. And I gather his partners value his business opinions. Market trends and such. But when he's in Mum's company he gets lost."

Willie looked sideways at Gill. "Does he seek solace elsewhere?"

"Oh I've no idea!" For a moment she was shocked. "Mind you, he has a faithful secretary who's been with him for years. I'd guess they're very close. She's quite attractive. Lilias Watson ... I really never thought about it, Willie."

Lex leaned across. "Hey, Willie, Tommy's got a book up fur the fuckin' Halliday!"

"The Halliday Literary Award, Tommy? That's something. Well done, china."

"Thanks, Willie. It'll no win."

"Why not? It's time they gave the leading prize to one of us," said Lex. The others voiced their congratulations.

Nettie Bell spoke: "It's £30,000 first prize. We could just do with that, so we could."

"What the hell's the title, Tommy?" asked Lex. "Is it a secret?"

"No, no. It's in the bookshops already."

"Well?"

The apparently reluctant author put down his pint glass. "*Those Shining Walls*. I can't imagine why they've short-listed it. The Halliday judges, I mean."

"Why's that, Tommy?"

"I don't know, Willie. It's just ... well, the Halliday winners are usually not too experimental, if you know what I mean. 'Walls' is on the strong side, a bit far out. Know what I mean?"

"Not exactly, Tommy, without reading it. Which I shall do without delay. Anyhow, bloody well done, boy! Maybe it'll shake up the English bloody literary establishment, eh?"

Lex grasped his right elbow with his left hand and made an aggressive thrusting gesture. "Aye, bugger the fuckin' Bloomsbury set! Right, Tommy?"

"Mebbe," was the characteristically morose reply.

"Whit's it aboot anyway?"

"Difficult to explain, Lex. You'll have to read it. It's no a Mills and Boon. Promise you that."

They were going to get no more out of Tommy Bell that night.


Willie's *Recorder* article leapt off the page:

## THE FUSE IS BURNING

I attended the patriotic demonstrations this week at the Scottish Assembly building in Edinburgh. Barring some silly hangers-on, these were decent Scots folk – some of them my personal professional friends – on the cold, drizzly streets. Their placards said it all: 'Free Scotland', 'Westminster – hands off', 'A Scottish Parliament for Scots', 'Independence Now!' They shouted and sang 'Flower of Scotland', a visionary light in their eyes.

But talking to these good people, I found the overwhelming mood to be one of heart-sickness with distant, unrepresentative, incompetent, uncaring English Government. They want change – soon! Don't we all want change, here in our beloved Scotland? Don't we want out of the accursed, obsolete Union? Don't we want to lay hold on our own destiny? Don't we want to manage our own affairs, directly, not at one remove? Don't we want to take our own dignified independent Scottish place in the European Parliament? Of course we do!

And yet, the blind politicians in the South continue to mistake Scots' respect for law and order, the lack, so far, of arson and broken glass, as signifying a less than eager national aspiration for independence. It is a dangerous delusion.

Alastair Dunn, 34, a schools equipment salesman and Nationalist supporter over from Dunfermline for the demonstrations, put it like this: "All the recent polls show we need our *own* government. If Labour go on insisting on devolution only and the Tories go on forcing the Union down our throats, I foresee trouble. There could be a hell of an explosion! And I mean literally. All over the place. I reckon the fuse is already burning!"

If Mr Dunn is right and violence, born of years of political frustration, should break out, the culprits will not be the steady, law-abiding Scottish people but the scandal-ridden, played-out clingers to office in Westminster who have long forgotten the meaning of the words vision or hope. But we in Scotland have not forgotten: we will not wait much longer for the satisfaction of our deepest national yearning for independence!

Gill rang Willie as soon as she'd seen the piece. It was eleven thirty on Saturday morning.

"Some article Willie! Isn't that the straight Scottish National Party line though?"

"No. Independence yes, but the rest is waffle."

"*Waffle?*"

"Yeah. Stirring folks up, but nothing too specific, if you read it carefully."

"But you're debunking the Labour and Conservative policies, so what does that leave?"

He coughed for about twenty seconds. Gill knew he'd just lit a cigarette. For a sentence or two his voice came in a whisper. "It leaves people scratching their heads and wondering if something unpleasant might happen. The odd MP might even get off his bum to try to check up on opinion up here. But I said nothing about the possible political *composition* of a future Scottish Parliament."

"Yes, I see," said Gill.

"Listen, sweetheart, meet me in the pub about half twelve. We'll have a pie or something and then come back here. I think there's a good Hindi film on the TV. Does that appeal?"

Gill was already hotly willing the next two hours to pass. "I'll be there, Willie love. Don't be late."

It was not to be: They spent a happy enough time in the Argyle with Lex, Mo and Hamish, ate their bar snacks, then walked back to Rubyvale Street in a barely controlled excitement. But a worried looking Mrs Skelly met them on the stair-head.

"The polis his been here, Mr Devine! Looking for you. You've tae phone yer editor at the office *immediate*. God, Mr Devine, I hope you're no in ony bother, like? The polis, them po-faced young bastarts, wouldnae say."

Willie laid his hand on her forearm. "Thanks, Mrs Skelly. There's no bother. It'll just be some technicality about news regulations they're wanting a word about."

"Technicalities ... aye that'll be it." She shuffled towards her door. "I bloody hope so onyweys."

But Gill did not mistake the sudden anxiety in Willie's eyes.

# FOUR

GILL WAITED, alternately watching TV, making cups of coffee and pacing round the room. About four thirty she decided to take a short walk outside. Once again Mrs Skelly waylaid her.

"Ony word yet, miss?"

"No, but I'm not worrying, Mrs Skelly. He'll be back soon I'm sure."

There were generations of suspicion and insecurity in the older woman's slumped shoulders and shaking head.

"I wouldnae trust the polis. They can aye twist the God's truth to suit theirsels." She lifted her head and glanced up the stair. "I'd be bloody sorry tae see Mr Devine awa'. He's a kind laddie, that Willie. I ken, see?"

The woman clearly wanted to say more. Gill responded, "Why d'you say that, Mrs Skelly?"

"Back there last winter I wis awfu' bad wi' the arthritis. In ma back, like. Couldnae get out t'dae ma messages or nothin'. Well, that Willie notices I'm lyin' doggo, so he chaps on the door and asks whit can he dae tae help."

"Oh well ..." Gill began.

"Naw, see, that might seem nothin' to a well brung up young lady like yoursel, miss. But roon here if you're oot the gemme like I wis, they're lookin' tae see if there's some wey they can rob youse. But no Willie Devine. Must hiv been weeks. Aye, aboot three weeks he did ma bit shoppin'. Every day I gied him a wee list in the morn and every night, regular as the church clock, he brung back the items. And a few times there wis an extra tin fur me, or some sweeties or

53

fags or something like that. Don't know whit I'd hiv done withoot Mr Devine, I'm tellin' you straight – Gill, is it no?"

"Yes, Mrs Skelly, that's me. I'm glad Willie gave you a hand. Look, I'm going down for a breath of air now. Don't worry, he'll be back in no time."

She was back in the flat at five fifteen. What could be happening? Willie was a journalist: surely the police couldn't charge him with anything? Britain was a land of free speech still, wasn't it? Might he be involved in something else? But what? Drugs, fraudulent financial dealings, break-ins? She knew he just didn't fit such profiles.

Gill gave up speculating. Her mind returned to Muirlaw Drive. What on earth must her father and mother have been saying to one another since her decampment last Sunday? Had they had a row?

They had.

Muriel was on her feet in the sitting room as soon as Robert returned from Jordanhill.

"I hope you feel proud of yourself, Bob?"

"Muriel, I think we should ..."

"I've never before seen such a spineless display, even from *you*."

Robert realized that his wife would now throw off all restraint. It was pointless to attempt a rational discussion in her present mood. He knew that. But he also accepted wearily that an argument was nevertheless unavoidable.

"I couldn't see the sense in aggravating things further, Muriel. Gill was clearly determined to go. Maybe it'll be for the best in the end."

"Ach, Bob, you're hopeless!"

"That's not fair. There was nothing we could realistically do. Gill's not a child and ..."

"Oh shut up! It's one thing for one's daughter to move out, to share a flat or whatever, when everything's been nicely arranged. But this unseemly exit is not like that, and I at least am not about to pretend it is."

Robert eyed his agitated wife, then said, "I'm afraid you're going to have to accept that it was you, Muriel, who drove Gill away."

"You *bastard*!" she screamed. "Our daughter brings some ill-mannered, ill-dressed guttersnipe into our beautiful house from God knows where and you react as if it's Mr Gibson the Minister on a visit. Rotten cowardice I call it! You don't change, do you, Bob?"

He lit a small cheroot, an indulgence normally confined to the garden or the office, and drew hard on it with a shaking hand. "Unless you can keep control, Muriel, and leave personal insult out of it, we'd best close this conversation *now*."

"Typical! Well then, nice Mr MacIntyre, please tell me why you couldn't show Mr Willie whatever-his-name-is what you thought of him. Why couldn't you make it clear that we have no time for his cheap lefty twaddle? That *we* intend to keep up standards?"

"Because, Muriel – one: I am not a snob, and never have been, and – two: because I am not at all convinced that what he was talking about was twaddle. No doubt some of it may have been extreme, and I don't pretend to know all the answers to Scotland's problems today, but ... well ..."

"Well what?"

"I just think one has to listen to the other man's point of view sometimes."

Muriel made a disgusted face. "Marvellous. That get's you right off the hook, doesn't it?" She struck out again. "Were you quite happy then to welcome that scum to Muirlaw Drive? Did you even *notice* the condition of his clothes? And on a Sunday visit, mind you."

"I'm afraid young folks aren't as concerned with appearances as we were, Muriel."

"Och, nonsense! *Decent* young people are just the same, allowing for changes of style of course. Look at Jamie Ballantyne."

Robert felt tired. "Jamie's certainly a bright young fellow, I must say." His cheroot was finished. "I'll have to go into the kitchen to stub this out, Muriel."

"Go on then. Duck the issue as usual. The story of your life, Bob."

Something constricted Robert's throat. Suddenly he was wildly angry. It didn't happen often. He rounded on his grimacing wife. "Get off my back, you moaning bitch! I tried to keep the peace today, to treat Willie Devine in a civilised manner. No, he's not our type, I grant you that. But he's my daughter's friend, for the moment anyway, and that's good enough for me. I ..."

"So you ... ?"

"Shut your face for once, woman! As I say, I acted today as a gentleman, I hope, in a difficult situation. But you, oh no! Mrs high and mighty MacIntyre isn't prepared to hear a word from anyone unless it's going to be according to her own particular script. So you just go ahead and abuse a guest and alienate our daughter. Wonderful!"

Muriel was white-faced. Her hands hung limply at her sides. "Bob, I ..."

He had not finished. "I'm sick and tired of your damned self-centredness, Muriel. You don't seem to care any more what you say, who you hurt. Who the hell do you think you are anyway? Lady MacThatcher or something? Well, just take it from me, Muriel, neither you nor I nor anyone else around here is any great shakes. We're simply middle-class, middle-aged folks doing what we can in life. So get off your high horse – for your own good."

For the second time that evening tears slid down Muriel MacIntyre's carefully powdered cheeks.

"Bob, I'm sorry if ..."

"Just go to bed, Muriel. I don't want to talk any more, not tonight anyway. I'll sleep in the spare room. Don't bother about breakfast: I'll deal with it in the morning."

"Oh, Bob. D'you think Gill will be all right?"

"Yes. Cathie Lonie seemed a good type. Now go upstairs. Just put a pair of pyjamas in the spare room, if you will, Muriel."

Meekly she closed the door and left him to his thoughts.

They'd had rows before. Not often – he hated this type of confrontation, always did everything he could to avoid an open clash. But, really, she was impossible at times. It wasn't that he didn't still admire Muriel, her strength of character, her pride, her poise. Sadly he reminded himself it was a long time since sexual intimacy had been a part of their life together, but the odd night, or occasionally an afternoon, with dear, devoted Lilias, his secretary, kept him content enough on that score. No, he and Muriel had a satisfactory married life, pursuing their own interests. Not an unusual pattern, if he read correctly between the lines of some of his golfing friends' conversations.

Why had Muriel been so bloody-minded with this Willie character? Class: undoubtedly that had been an element. She'd not welcomed the man's obvious imperviousness to the niceties of afternoon tea etiquette, those little politenesses which meant so much to her and her kind. That he'd made no attempt to dress at least a little smartly for the occasion, especially for a first meeting, had outraged her. It was like a slap in the face, a two-fingered gesture to the gentility of Muriel's world. Robert decided that it had not been wholly unreasonable, if damned awkward, for Muriel to react as she had, up to a point anyway.

He looked round the room. In the far corner their Danemann upright, open *Mikado* score in place. Muriel still played tolerably well. He'd used to enjoy singing 'Tit Willow' to her accompaniment when friends came round, in the early days. His party piece. In small arched alcoves above either side of the fireplace stood finely carved chinese jade figurines. On the wall behind him hung Muriel's prize possession, a small original Rennie Mackintosh flower drawing, framed in gilt bamboo. Flanking an attractively coloured heavy Caithness glass bowl, atop a central coffee table, lay current copies of *Country Life* and *Scottish Field* magazines. At one end of the window sill an earthenware pot of gracefully cascading chlorophytum was stationed, at the other one of Muriel's own sculpted terra cotta miniatures, a nude young girl in the act of diving. Below the sill in a mahogany glass-topped display case was her collection of silver-fitted Scottish rams' horn snuff mulls. Soft light spilled from the ormolu standard lamp's Tiffany shade onto the carpet which was an unusual woven blend of subtle greens, blues and ochre. The Tientsin rug in front of the fireplace glowed, an opulent crimson. Robert was well aware of, and much appreciated, his wife's artistic good taste.

He could quite see that Willie Devine's peremptory introduction into Muriel's lovingly created ambience had inevitably brought forth a defensive reaction. But, in the past, she'd not been so downright hostile. He thought of Gill's elder sister Fiona, and some of her early swains – long-haired, dirty-fingernailed individuals who would clear a plate of shortbread when they'd hardly got in the door! Muriel had actually seen the funny side of those visits, and they'd both had a good laugh. So why had she behaved so abominably today?

Of course it was Devine's obvious political attitude. That was the difference from those others. Robert tried to recall accurately what Willie had said. Was it just the familiar Socialist line – down with the Tories, up with the working class; throw out the bosses, put trade unionists on Boards of Directors; outlaw private education; soak the rich by increasing wealth taxes – and so on down the weary list? Not really. In any case, the Labour Party's policies in many of those areas had been considerably modified in recent times. So what had he actually said which had caught Muriel on the raw?

Well, certainly he'd not been prepared to share her wholesale denunciation of all Socialists, Labour councillors and the like. And her slighting references to Roman Catholics couldn't have helped, even if he had lost his faith. But it was Willie's clear objection to the Westminster set-up and his remarks about the need for radical change that had really got Muriel going. Robert knew his wife's ultra-conservative nature and now, carefully recollecting the afternoon's events, he realized that this had been the true source of her discomfiture.

For they had both already learned from the articles which Gill had shown them that Willie was overtly in favour of Scotland's withdrawal from the 1707 Treaty of Union with England and the setting up of an independent parliament in Edinburgh. Not some half-way house devolved assembly, but a full-blown government with tax-raising powers and defense responsibilities. And this was the notion to which Muriel was so implacably opposed.

What did he, Robert MacIntyre, 53, stockbroker in the City of Glasgow and, as he regarded himself anyway, from the solid middle of the West of Scotland's middle class – what did he think? First of all, he wished profoundly that he didn't have to consider the matter at all. Keeping up with the volatile markets absorbed most of his mental energies. He flattered himself that he was not unskilled at calling price changes, trend reversals, chart breakout points. He kept his ear close to the ground, was constantly reading the financial journals and watching the screens in the dealing room. He didn't miss much, but it left him little time for political questions.

But Robert did know that there was discontent in Scotland. Inevitable, really, with the London-based Government's majority coming from the opposite party to that overwhelmingly voted for north of the border. But did he really think that a break with England was now desirable, or necessary?

In his younger days the Nationalists had never really made any impact. Beards, sandals and bagpipes. The business community had never taken their case seriously, nor had the Labour Party, whatever they said. And the Tories were, after all, the Unionist Party. But things had changed quite evidently in the two countries, and the European Community had developed enormously since those days. Then there was North Sea oil. Probably a much more respectable economic case for independence could be made now.

But what about business confidence in a Scotland cut adrift from the United Kingdom? How would potential American and Japanese industrial investors react? And, most importantly, would the net result be a negative Socialist administration in Edinburgh for ever and a day? That was what terrified Muriel. She was not really a selfish, acquisitive woman who was insensitive to the demands of the needy, but a certain style in life was meat and drink to her. And she did not see that sort of style being favoured or perhaps even permitted, in any conceivable future socialist utopia in Scotland.

Robert got up, switched off the light and went upstairs to the spare bedroom. He'd have to patch things up with Muriel tomorrow evening. Perpetuating a quarrel was valueless from both their points of view. As he undressed he recognized that he had not come to any worthwhile conclusions. Perhaps he'd accurately defined the underlying cause of today's explosion, but this question of the country's political direction was fraught with so many imponderables that he wasn't readily going to form any clear opinion about it. God! he really didn't need those kind of problems. There was enough to contend with at the office. Was Muriel also trying to get her thoughts straight, he wondered, as he drifted into sleep?

She was. The whole day had been shattering, ending with Gill's completely unexpected departure and an unpleasant contretemps with Bob. Was she, Muriel MacIntyre, 48, housewife, mother and part-time artist living in Bearsden, was she to blame? Maybe she had been a a bit sharp, not to say rude, with that damned journalist, but that was the only way one got through to that type. In her experience they had skins like rhinoceroses. But Muriel made no attempt to analyse what anyone had actually said: she couldn't get out of her mind the look of sheer anger in her daughter's eyes just before she left.

As Muriel too fell into a fitful sleep she decided what she'd do next day. Janey Smith wanted to see her about the notelet drawings: she'd drop in at the gift shop and ask for Janey's advice. She was such a dear and so level-headed. Discreet too.

And so, over a glass of sherry, crackers and mackerel paté in Janey Smith's snug little back shop during the lunch hour closure, Muriel recounted all that had happened the day before.

"What age is this man, Muriel?"

"Thirty five, I believe. He's not unattractive, in a sort of basic way. Good features. Clearly intelligent. Manly enough. But cussed, Janey. Bolshie. And simply no idea of how to dress, you know ... for a visit on a Sunday afternoon. That blue-jean navvy rig may be acceptable these days in newspaper offices, but it's quite of place in Muirlaw Drive."

Janey was a shrewd, strongly built, slow moving woman. Her

bosom was full in her Pringle twin-set, her fine tweed skirt pleasingly moulded about her lower person. Her broad face habitually gave away little of her inner thoughts. "Uh-huh. I can imagine, Muriel. Difficult for you. Have you seen anything of what he writes?".

"Oh yes, Janey. Rabble-rousing left wing stuff. Damn the Tories and all that. With a heavy dash of that Nationalist rubbish."

"He's on that bandwagon, is he?"

"Well and truly. I can't *imagine* what Gill sees in him."

Janey topped up their Amontillado. "I shouldn't worry, dear. Those sort of attractions at Gill's age generally don't last. I expect it's fun to slum it a bit before you have to contemplate the hard realities of life and settle down."

"Yes, I know and I wish it were like that, but I don't think so, I'm afraid." Suddenly the bleak fact of Gill's angry leaving closed in on Muriel again. Since getting up that morning she'd stayed busy, but now, relaxing, she couldn't keep the misery of yesterday evening at bay any longer. She felt tearful. "Just between us, Janey, she's left home."

"What, yesterday?"

"Yes, gone to a colleague's flat in Jordanhill. She said she'll be in touch, but I've no idea when. Or whether she'll want to. With *me* anyway." Muriel dabbed her now moist eyes.

Janey frowned sympathetically. "What does Bob say about it?"

Muriel sniffed. "We had a bad row. Bob's a good husband but he's weak when it comes to this sort of thing. I get no support, Janey."

She sniffed again. Janey leant forward and patted her hand solicitously.

"Now, now, Muriel dear. Tell me, did you actually cross swords with this chap? I mean ... on political matters?"

"I most certainly did! He was telling us that all those awful Labour councils are public-spirited angels who would do splendid jobs if only Westminster didn't deprive them of funds – of which, by the way, there is apparently no shortage whatsoever."

"That's damned nonsense, Muriel."

"Not according to Mr William Devine, Janey. Anyhow, his solution is to pull Scotland out of the United Kingdom and install his lefty friends in an independent parliament in Edinburgh. Can you imagine what life would be like, permanently under that lot?"

"In a word, Muriel, yes. I suppose he'd grab all the oil revenues, to finance the spending spree?"

"No doubt." The sherry had calmed Muriel. The fight went out of her. She needed comforting. "Janey, am I wrong to love my house and our possessions? I mean, it's not an obsession but I can't bear to think of losing them."

"I'm sure, but no government is likely to do that sort of thing, is it?"

"Not immediately, but there would be higher taxes I don't doubt, and especially wealth taxes, whatever the Socialists might say at first to get voted in. And what price private schooling? Charitable status?" She sipped her drink and accepted another cream cracker. "Bob and I have worked hard to build up our life and I want to be able to pass things on. I ..." Her voice faltered. "Maybe Fiona and Gill don't *want* anything from us, Janey ... Oh God!"

Muriel dissolved in tears.

She was sitting on a small chintz sofa. Janey came over and sat beside her. "My dear girl, you're very upset, aren't you." She took Muriel's hand.

Muriel sobbed. "Oh Janey, I'm so miserable! I don't know where to turn. The children don't seem to be part of me any longer. Bob and I are hardly ever on net. Our marriage is, well, you know ... really a bit hollow." She sobbed.

Janey put her arm round her distressed friend and squeezed her reassuringly. "Don't take it so hard, Muriel. I do understand but ..."

"I just feel hopeless!" Muriel blurted out. "About politics, artistic standards, morality – oh, everything! I seem to be out of step all the time. I simply can't understand things any more. What's wrong with me, Janey?"

"Nothing, my dear. You're in good company, I assure you. But we have to soldier on, don't we? Somehow, or we go under, Muriel."

Muriel MacIntyre couldn't remember the last time she'd had a good cry. She let go now. Weeping without attempting any further talk, she thankfully laid her head on Janey's warm breast and let her stroke her hair and forehead. Despite her distraught state, Muriel fleetingly recalled rumours of Janey's special relationship with a younger woman who'd lived with her in Milngavie for some years. She didn't care: Janey was being kind and that was all that mattered to Muriel. Eventually she regained control, took out her compact and repaired the damage to her complexion as best she could. She blew her nose vigorously.

"I married too young, Janey. Hardly out of the Glasgow Art School. I should have had a proper career, travelled a bit. Widened my horizons. Ah well!"

"You and Bob have been on holiday all over the place. Morocco, South Africa, Canada. I've often envied you."

"That's not the same," said Muriel curtly, now fully in charge of herself again.

They discussed final plans for the notelet illustrations. Then it was shop reopening time.

"Are you feeling better, dear?"

"I am, Janey. Thanks for putting up with me and my stupid problems."

"They're not stupid, Muriel. And some of them affect me too, you know. Anyway, keep smiling!"

They embraced in sisterly solidarity and, when they drew apart, Janey placed her index finger under Muriel's chin and grinned at her. Muriel grinned back.

But driving home, she felt as confused as ever about Willie Devine and all he seemed to stand for. Maybe her rigid adherence to the political status quo should be jettisoned. She was as patriotic a Scotswoman as any other. Of course she was. But that didn't mean that she had to welcome proposals for *any* constitutional change, just for the sake of it. Certainly not if it was going to lead to Daddy's

'Cloth Cap Brigade's' ruling the roost for the foreseeable future. Oh no! But surely that would be exactly the result of independent status for Scotland?

By the time she reached Muirlaw Drive Muriel's puzzled depression was threatening again. A very strong cup of tea was called for.

By six o'clock Gill was becoming alarmed at Willie's continued absence, when he walked in. She flew to him.

"Willie! I thought you were never coming."

"Blame the paranoid police."

"What did they want?"

"What did they *not* want? Christ!" He sat down, looking exhausted.

"Will I make some tea?"

"No. There's a bottle of Standfast in the press there, Gill. I could do with a good dram."

"Right. Come to, then tell me about it."

They both drank silently.

"Aw, that's better," he said, combing back his hair with his fingers. "Well, the bastards wanted every wee detail of yours truly's existence to date. Family members' names, ages, sexes, occupations. My father's life story, my old mother's present address. Whether I had a 'partner' and, if so, all her, or his, details."

"What did you say on the last point?"

"That I was a misogynous bachelor. So, don't worry, wee hen, you're not known to the fuckin' boys in blue."

"Did they grill you on your political views?"

"Oh aye. Naturally. That was what it was all about. That's what took the time."

"I suppose they'd seen your recent article? The one on the Scottish Assembly building demos."

"Right, and they didn't like it."

"Too provocative or what?"

"Verging on 'incitement to violence', according to them. Crap!"

"How did you argue?"

"Exactly as I wrote. That the demonstrations were remarkable for their *lack* of violent protest. That the demonstrators were good law-abiding citizens."

Gill sipped her whisky thoughtfully. "But you did say something about the possibility of violence if political change doesn't come, now didn't you, Willie?"

"Indeed I did, and I have no intention of retracting any of that. But what I wrote was absolutely not an incitement to violence. In my book it was 'an incitement to political reform'. Not exactly the same thing, you must admit."

"Doesn't matter what I think, Willie."

"It bloody well does to me, Gill!"

She examined his face. Beneath the assured look she thought she detected an uncharacteristic nervousness. Like any Glaswegian, Gill knew well the reputation of the city's police force. Willie had probably been through the mill.

"Did you persuade them then?"

"No. They were not interested in the truth. They never are, those bastards. Just set on achieving their pre-agreed objective."

"Which was?"

"To put the fear of Holy Christ up me." He threw back his drink. "Give me some more of that, sweetheart."

"What else did they want to know, Willie?"

"Och, who all my associates are. Any specific political affiliations, etcetera et bloody cetera. Pain in the fuckin' arse. Oh and they were curious about that wee salesman, Alastair Dunn. The one in the demo article. What did I know about his activities?"

"And?"

"I said he was just an imaginary figure, a mouthpiece for what I had to say. A journalistic device."

"I thought he was a real person."

"He is."

"So how could you ... ?"

"Gill, Gill, we have to protect our sources. Right? Well, I couldn't see any sense in dragging poor Mr Dunn into this. Cross-questioning in Dunfermline Police HQ. He's just an ordinary wee guy."

"Wasn't that risky? They might check."

"Maybe. I doubt it. He's small fry."

"You're big fry?"

"Obviously. But never mind. Sandy Black, the Editor, was able to show them a draft for Tuesday's article. A relatively innocuous piece about absentee landlords not culling deer properly, planting too many conifers. Environmental issues, even if there is a political edge to it."

"And that satisfied them?"

"I think it annoyed them, because they couldn't reasonably object. Anyway, they pissed off after that. That was when the real argy-bargy began."

"With Mr Black?"

"Aye. You can imagine. 'Willie, you'll have to soft pedal your column. Cut down on overt criticism of the Government, the authorities. Concentrate on other issues a bit more'. And so on."

"Did you not agree?"

"No. I told him he'd have to let me write what I want, along the same lines as before, or he could stick the job. He's a yellow creep, but he knows what sells papers."

"Did he concede?"

"With a bad grace. So I won, but I'll have to be a bit fly for a while, Gill." He held out his glass. "Be a good girl and pour me another drop. Then come over here and give Willie a great big cuddle."

Gill complied with both requests. Soon the hazards of hard-hitting journalism were forgotten as they crab-walked from the kitchen into the bedroom, hugging and kissing fiercely. In minutes they were on the bed, urgently pulling off each other's clothes. Willie tugged down Gill's tights. He buried his face in her belly. He stuck his tongue in her navel, slid his lips slowly upwards over her quivering skin until he reached her breasts. The nipples stood erect for his kisses. Gill groaned in rapidly mounting hunger. She felt the eager rigidity of his penis in the palm of her hand and guided him into a glorious penetration. They bent to mutual lovemaking with a will.

Afterwards they slept for a little. Around nine they cooked bacon, eggs and some black pudding Gill had bought. They each ate an apple and were enjoying coffee when there was a knock at the door. Gill raised her eyebrows enquiringly but Willie shook his head, getting up to see who it was.

"Oh hello, Danny! Come in. Gill, this is Danny Ramage, an old friend and sometime fellow boozer. Right, Danny?"

They laughed easily together.

"Can I get you a coffee, Danny. Or maybe some whisky?"

"Coffee would be great, Gill. Ta." He turned to Willie. "I was wanting a word but if it's no convenient I'll ..."

"No, that's OK, Danny. Come and sit over here at the table. Gill can put the telly on."

There was a moderately interesting documentary film on about the social lives of Amazonian tree-frogs, but Gill felt wounded by Willie's attitude. She couldn't avoid hearing some of the information being conveyed by the surprisingly high-voiced Danny Ramage. Willie had started to scribble in his reporter's notebook.

"All set then ... the gear's all in and tested ... van's ready ... picked a time when there's few workers on duty ... aye, it's the General Post Office in George Square – symbolic, know what I mean? ... the Easter Rising and that."

Gill stood up. "I'm going out for a few minutes," she said. "Won't be long."

Willie looked round, frowning interrogatively, but she slipped out quickly and closed the door. She walked unhappily up and down the main street. However, it was a chilly night and she soon went back. Ramage had gone.

"What was all that about, Willie, if you don't mind my asking?"

He leaned down and kissed her on the cheek. "You can ask, Gill love, but I'm not going to tell you. In this job, if you're any good, people confide in you because they think maybe you can help. And that kind of information is like gold dust. But it will just blow away if you turn out to be a blether, a blabbermouth who can't be trusted."

"But, Willie! I mean, it's *me* who's asking."

"*No-one* gets told. No betrayals. It's hard, I know, but that's the rule. Mine anyhow."

Gill made an impatient face. "I consider that jolly unfair. I was allowed to sit here and I couldn't help overhearing Danny. It sounded to me like some sort of conspiracy being cooked up."

"You heard nothing, Gill. *Nothing*, d'you understand?"

"Well, perhaps I do and perhaps I don't. Listen, Willie, I won't press you but I love you and I'm worried. Something dangerous is brewing. I feel it in my bones. Promise me you're not getting involved."

He put his arms round her. "I've told you before, my profession is journalism – observing, analysing and reporting. That's my only 'involvement'."

She put her face close to his and looked into his eyes. "Promise?"

"Yes," he said with utter seriousness. Then he slapped her playfully on the bottom. "Get your coat and away home with you, my lassie. It's late. I've some writing to do."

Gill was being dismissed. Like other members of her family, she did not sleep well that night. What a strange day it had been. When she and Willie had been making love, wondrous, energetic, frantic, soaring, obliterating physical love, she'd never felt so close to another human being, she doubted if she ever would again. And yet a couple of hours later she'd known the anguished sensation of being excluded from the inner sanctum of his life, that dynamic intellectual and emotional powerhouse which drove Willie Devine, and which Gill suspected to be the true source of his attraction for her. Could she tolerate such an ambivalent status?

## FIVE

GILL TOOK TWO messages at school on the Monday, the first by telephone. It was Jamie Ballantyne.

"Hi, Gill! How are you? Hope it's OK ringing you at school?"

"It's all right, Jamie. I'm fine, thanks."

"I heard from your Mum you'd moved to a flat. I rang a few times on Saturday, but you were out. Then yesterday I was at the office till late with the interior decorating people. We're just about done. Open for biz next week."

"Congratulations, Jamie. What about your flat?"

"Likewise. I'm living there now – among the paint pots and rolls of wallpaper. Smartening it up a bit. Quite fun!" He laughed breezily. "Listen, Gill, the big wheel's coming up from London on Friday for a small opening celebration, at the Sheridan Hotel, private suite. Our banker, the solicitor, and a few of the bigger clients, booked and prospective."

"Very nice. Well done, Jamie."

"I was wondering if you'd be my partner for the evening? You know, kind of hostess. I think you'd enjoy it, Gill. And I'd appreciate your help very much, needless to add. What d'you say?"

Gill hesitated. How should she react? Jamie was an old friend and she could see that her presence would genuinely help him. She liked him too. His progress in business was interesting. But if she agreed, was she sending him an unintended signal? Truthfully, her whole mind was full of Willie. She simply didn't want any other male company. But then, yesterday she'd not been able to see her lover: he'd been too occupied with various meetings. She *should* maintain some sort of independent social life, shouldn't she? It was 1995 and Gillian MacIntyre was a fully liberated woman, wasn't she? Friday was always a busy night for Willie, ahead of his column on Saturday.

"That sounds intriguing, Jamie. I'd love to come. The Sheridan, you say?"

"Yes. That's great, Gill! Thanks a million. I'll pick you up at, say, six at the Jordanhill address? Fill you in about the attendees on the way in. OK?"

"Lovely, Jamie. What should I wear – ball gown or jeans?"

His bellow of laughter was boyish, infectious.

"Something just a wee bit formal, Gill. Sort of cocktail dress?"

"Fine. I'll be ready."

"We should be through by nine latest. I'd like to take you for a quiet supper somewhere afterwards. Have a bit of a chat."

"Super! Right then, till Friday. 'Byee."

Gregory V Abrahams, Jnr., was the American head of Mekay & Schwartz's London office, charged with expansion into Europe. Following Paris and Geneva, Glasgow was his newest venture. Jamie told Gill that he had 'hit it off from the word go' with Mr Abrahams and that he, Jamie, had been the one to persuade him to open in Scotland. "So I have to make it work, Gill." Buchanan, their banker, would be there, and Milroy, the lawyer. "Alec Beattie's the advertising capo at Kirkwood Turner the whisky people – you know, 'Ptarmigan' brand."

Gill was impressed. "That's a big account, isn't it, Jamie?"

"Rather! He's our star attraction. 'Course, we can only hope for a *share* of his budget. Then there's Bill Jones from Kumfitred, the carpet and floor tile manufacturers. John Abercrombie of Sinclair Foods. They've got a big contract with British Airways. They also supply Icelandair and Air Canada. Real goer, John, it seems. Jeremy Nathan's coming too. His outfit is fairly substantial in fine stationery, gift writing packs, that type of thing. I haven't actually met him myself yet. And my secretary, on trial, Charlotte Cholmondley-Pickersgill."

"Charlotte *who*?"

"Cholmondley-Pickersgill. Yes, it is a bit of a handle, isn't it? Charlotte's English."

"No! I don't believe you."

They laughed.

"She had the most interesting CV, and she's decidedly decorative. Necessary for the reception desk in our line, Gill."

They collected Mr Abrahams, from his suite, an amiable, slim, silver-haired, bespectacled sixty year old New Yorker. This professorial appearance was however contradicted by a purple suit, green suede moccasins and a screaming orange silk tie.

"Wow! Dig that tie," said Jamie straight away, lifting it out horizontal for inspection.

Mr Abrahams beamed. "Well now, Jamie, that's nice of you to say so."

Jamie tucked the tie back in place. Gill could see that he knew how to handle his boss.

"Say, this must be Gill? I'm glad to meet you, Gill. I'll be right happy if you'll call me Greg. OK?"

"Right, I will, Greg. Thank you."

The private room was a penthouse suite with a long view over the Clyde and the city's lights.

"Say, this is just like home, Jamie!"

"You like it, Greg? Good. It's not all mountains and mist up here, you know. Now, give me a moment while I check up on the drinks and eats." He went over to the waiters manning a long white table-clothed bar.

"You've some interesting people coming tonight, Greg," said Gill.

"Sure have, Gill. I've got to hand it that young man there. He doesn't let the grass grow. I picked him for a winner first time I saw him. In New York that was, 'bout three years ago."

They moved over to a huge window and studied the view. Gill did her best to point out such landmarks as were floodlit.

Jamie rejoined them with three glasses. "Everything seems to be under control. Here's a drop of bubbly. Greg, would you like to propose a toast?"

"Right on! Several. To the great success of Mekay & Schwartz (Scotland), and to the future career of its talented manager. But I want to join that to the health and happiness of our charming hostess here."

"You're the only one who can drink to all three, Greg!" said Jamie.

"Oh, is that right? Yeah, I guess so. Well ..."

"To hell with modesty! We're in the hype game, aren't we?" said Jamie. "I'm going to drink with you, Greg. You too, Gill. Cheers – here's to tonight as well." They drank. "And another toast. To Greg Abrahams, without whose vision and courage none of this would be happening. Gill?"

The American flushed with obvious pleasure.

Charlotte did not arrive, she made an entrance. Her shortish brunette hair was attractively coiffed and she was dramatically made-up with dark coral lipstick and liberal eye-shadow. Large gold hooped earrings swung about her neck. Her obviously healthy, sinuously tall figure was clad in an emerald one-piece garment, caught in at the ankles and reminiscent of the harem. Her neat waist was encircled by a gold belt and on her feet were a pair of soft slippers, also of a gold material.

"Good evening, everybody!" this apparition greeted them. "Jamie, my sweet boss, I'm freezing!"

So saying she advanced towards Jamie and enfolded him in an extravagant embrace. He disengaged himself quickly, looking sheepish.

"This is Charlotte, Gill. Charlotte Cholmondley-Pickersgill, Gillian MacIntyre."

"I've heard about you, Gill," said Charlotte expressionlessly, turning abruptly away after shaking hands. "And *you* must be Mr Gregory Abrahams, sir?"

"Yeah, Charlotte, that's me."

Did she curtsy? She might have.

"Then I'm honoured and absolutely delighted." She offered her hand, which the American awkwardly kissed.

The man's essential banality, beneath the garish sartorial disguise, was painful as he stated flatly, "Pleased t'meet you, I'm sure."

Guests arrived in quick succession. Gill began to wonder if she was to have any real function as Charlotte swooped among the men like a great tropical bird. They vied to speak to her, to stand close to this gorgeous houri with large green eyes and alarmingly long white, scarlet-tipped fingers. Gill thought that Mr Jeremy Nathan, who had turned out to be an unexpected five foot blue-black giggling elf of South Indian origin, would faint with pleasure as Charlotte set about teasing him.

"I expect you've got *dozens* of wives, Mr Nathan."

"Oh no, oh no! It's not allowed."

"Well, lovely lady friends then." Momentarily her thinly-clad breasts brushed his shoulder.

"My goodness! What a naughty thing to say, Miss Charlotte." He giggled again and risked a quick pat to her long arm. "We are a Christian family. Oh yes."

But by then the exotic secretary had moved on to paralyse whatever talk had been taking place between Messrs. Milroy, the solicitor, and Jones, the carpet man.

Champagne flowed. Warm dishes and canapés circulated. Perhaps some of the men guests decided that Charlotte's conversation was not quite up to her appearance, but Gill found herself the object of increasing attention. Jamie had explained that this first party was being kept small, so that wives had not been bidden on this occasion.

"No, Mr Buchanan, Jamie and I are just old friends. Now, you're the firm's banker, isn't that right?"

"Yes, we are, Gill. And you? A career girl?"

"Teacher."

"Tough job these days."

The food manufacturer came over.

"Mr Abercrombie. Is your drink all right?"

"Yes, my dear. Just fine." He was rather elderly, a mite weak in the humour department, Gill guessed. "Must be careful. I'm driving."

Kumfitred Jones chipped in, "I've got the chauffeur the night. These advertising do's are usually good. But you cannae be too careful. That no right, Gill?" He winked ambiguously. Up through the ranks, Mr Jones, she reckoned.

Jamie joined them. "Gill knows Willie Devine on the *Recorder*. The columnist," he added. Keep the conversation moving: that was rule number one for a successful party.

"Devine?" said Buchanan sharply. "Isn't he the one who's always agin the Government and banging on about pulling out of the UK?"

"Yes, that's Willie, Mr Buchanan," said Gill.

"Well, maybe he's your friend, girl, but I can tell you we at the bank consider that a lot of tosh."

Jones cleared his throat noisily. He was a corpulent individual and probably didn't breathe too easily, thought Gill. "I know whit you mean, Mr Buchanan, but things are changing. I mean the polls asking folks' attitude about Devolution and Independence and all that, well, I mean, the results is quite different now from barely ten years ago. Isn't that so? I mean like fifty per cent, plus, are in favour o' a constitutional change."

"Ach, polls," replied the banker dismissively.

"No, but ..."

Jones was interrupted by John Abercrombie. "Bill's right. He and I are in the same Chamber and ..."

"Aye, so we are," confirmed Bill Jones.

"And, eh, well, the whole opinion in the area of sovereignty, an independent assembly for Scotland in Edinburgh and so on has swung right round among the membership. I would say Thatcher was the catalyst."

Buchanan was going to hold his position. "I am aware that some in the business community have decided to take that view. To support Devolution, but I wonder how many of them have taken the trouble to work out the economics of such a development?"

"Do I hear 'Devolution'?"

The speaker was Alec Beattie, the Ptarmigan Brand Whisky representative. Garbed in a smart denim suit, maroon polo-sweater and crocodile shoes, he was very much Gill's notion of an advertising executive. Alec was younger than most of the others.

"That's right, Alec," said Jamie. "We appear to have got into a political debate."

"Not too surprising, Jamie," responded the urbane Beattie. "One hears little else on all sides these days."

"Mr Buchanan strenuously dissenting," – Jamie shot the banker a disarming smile – "The consensus seems to be for Devolution. Quite unexpected ... really."

"Devolution will get us nowhere, gentlemen," said Beattie. "Neither fish nor fowl. A botched half-way house with insufficient powers to do any real good for Scotland. Forever looking over its shoulder to Westminster for permission, or approval. Useless."

"So you're for the present system with unrepresentative government in bloody London and chronic unemployment in Scotland and, the prime industrial contracts going to firms in South East England – is that whit you favour, Mr Beattie?" Bill Jones thrust out his fleshy chin.

Beattie smiled smoothly. "I said nothing of the kind. What I do say, however, is that either we take steps to improve our system of representation and strengthen Local Government's role *within* the Union – I mean, give the current arrangements an overhaul and then back them wholeheartedly, *or* – abrogate the Treaty, negotiate Independence once and for all, then get on with governing ourselves and *stop bickering*! Devolution is no solution."

There was an awkward silence, followed by mumbled confused comments: "Far too extreme," "Something in what he says," "Easy to talk."

Charlotte glided across. She'd held the company's rather staid lawyer and Greg Abrahams in thrall for some time.

"Mr Milroy and Mr Abrahams would like to rejoin the mainstream." She rolled her eyes for no readily identifiable reason.

"We need some more champagne, Charlotte," Jamie commanded sibilantly. "Wake up that steward. And more squash for Mr Nathan here."

Buchanan spoke again: "Mr Abrahams, what's the American view about nation states? You'll have heard there's a renewed demand, in *certain* quarters, for a Scottish Parliament? Even for separation from the United Kingdom?"

"Yeah, I heard something, but I don't believe I'm qualified to say. 'Ceptin' it's kinda hard to see what you'd want to change. I mean with your gracious Queen Elizabeth there in Bucking*ham* Palace and your fine government tradition an' all. Looks a dandy set-up from where I'm sitting."

Jamie quickly intervened: "I think the main complaint, Greg, is that London is too far away to be properly in touch with Scottish needs."

The American laughed. "Gee whiz, Jamie! It's not much above four hundred miles. One hour it took me by air. Washington to LA's twenty five hundred miles and *we* manage OK. Plus we got better 'n five times Britain's population."

Further inconclusive mumbles ensued. "No comparison to be drawn," "Look at the state of US politics today anyway," "A matter of Scottish identity in the end," "Maybe we *should* take a leaf out of the Yanks' federal book…"

Eventually they all left, Charlotte from the hotel forecourt in a thunderous Porsche driven by one Guy Beaumont, 'My latest glamorous escort'. The function had been a success. Jamie expressed himself a little anxious that politics had reared its head. "Still, maybe that will make the occasion stick in their minds. We're on the map now. That's the main thing."

Gill enquired about Mr Abrahams. "Should you not have asked him to come with us, Jamie?"

"No. Old Greg was champing at the bit to get off. Didn't you notice?"

"Can't say I did. Where's he off to?"

"Back to room 104, I should think. Arthur, the Hall Porter, has his instructions and a specification of what's required. Greg will be quite happy."

"I see. Is he married?"

"Wife number three. You should see her. Built like a battleship, voice like a foghorn. Really an awful specimen. Makes his life hell when she's in London."

"Why doesn't he divorce her too?"

"I gather he's working on it. But I suppose it gets expensive, third time round. Come on, I've booked a table at Luigi's Joint, the new Italian restaurant out by Anniesland. Have you been yet, Gill?"

"No, but I've heard of it, Jamie. Sounds great."

"Right, the car's down below. Let's go. Only snag is I'll have to stay on the *acqua minerale*. Disaster if I lost my licence."

The restaurant was full of cheerful chattering diners. The waiters, Glasgow Italians mainly, dashed hither and thither, shouting over the hubbub and holding dishes high above their heads. Jamie and Gill both ordered *fusilli alla Napoletana* and fell joyfully on the steaming food.

"This is fun, Jamie," said Gill, genuinely grateful.

"It is, isn't it?, Gill. We should do it more often."

She put down her fork. "Jamie, I hope I've made it clear that ..."

"Enough!" He held up a hand, palm outwards. "Don't please start talking about old Willie. I realize the situation. But we can still enjoy ourselves, Gill, can't we?"

"Of course, Jamie."

They ate in silence for a while. Then Jamie said, "Incidentally, thanks again for your help at the party."

"I didn't do much. Didn't need to with that secretary of yours rushing around. She's *colourful*, Jamie."

"I doubt she'll stay the course."

"Oh?"

"Well, as you'd gather, she hasn't much in the top storey." He tapped his head. "If she's the flame that attracts the business moths, then fair enough. But that phase will pass."

"I understand. What's her background?"

"Her father's a General, on a posting up here. For some reason. In Edinburgh actually, but Charlotte's been living with some character here in Glasgow and seems to have got to like it. Her parents own a large spread down in Sussex somewhere, I believe."

"One of our 'white settlers' then?"

"I always think that's a rather idiotic expression, Gill."

"It's how a lot of people feel."

Jamie shrugged disdainfully. "Whingeing Scots. If they don't like the English taking jobs and running businesses up here why don't they get off their bottoms and do something themselves? Show some initiative instead of bellyaching."

"I think one of the gripes is that the incomers have sold houses in the South at big prices, which puts them in a position to outbid the locals for small businesses, village shops, boarding houses in the holiday areas and so on."

"I bet that's only half the story most times, Gill. There are grants for business startups, you know. You can do it if you really want to, instead of just sitting around moaning. The thing is that Scots with that kind of energy have been leaving the country for years. It's the dregs who stay at home."

Gill took a mouthful of the house dry white. This was certainly different music from what she'd been hearing lately.

"That's a bit hard, Jamie. Not *everyone* who wants to get on can just up sticks and leave. In any case, why should our people *have* to leave?"

"Small country. Not enough opportunities."

"Maybe also economic mismanagement, Jamie? Not here, but by a distant administration that's not in touch with Scotland's requirements. If there was control here, there could be more hands-on planning. Why should we sit and watch while South East England gets all the attention? There are statistics to show..."

"Och hell, Gill!" Jamie interrupted. "Leave it out. I'm getting sick of all that stuff. Keep the dialectics for friend Willie. Right? Let us enjoy ourselves." He blew her a kiss across the table and smiled. "What d'you usually do for holidays?"

"Nothing too spectacular the last year or two. I walked the West Highland Way. Toured around Brittany with some friends from university."

"Once I've got the office running I'm thinking of grabbing ten days or so in the Caribbean. I've not been. Always wanted to. Snorkelling, corals, all that."

"Sounds like paradise, especially at this time of year, Jamie."

"Probably won't be till the autumn." He looked directly at her. "I wouldn't like to go alone, Gill."

Alarm bells were ringing. She really mustn't lead him on. "I hope you make it, Jamie," she said in a neutral tone. "Of course, I'm afraid I'll be slaving away over a hot timetable at that time of year."

He decided not to push. "Yes, I know. Well, anyway, I'll let you know if I can see a space. What about some *tiramisu*?"

"Lovely. Yes please."

They parted amicably at Gill's front door in Jordanhill, but without any arrangement to meet again beyond Jamie's vague remark as he got back into the Mercedes that, "You must come up some time to see the flat when it's finished." Jamie Ballantyne considered himself a canny operator.


Earlier that week at school Gill had just finished her last class and was proceeding along a corridor to the staff room when Sally Hughes met her.

"Oh, Gill there's a Major Colquhoun out in the front hall waiting to see you. Very grand, wearing a deerstalker."

"Goodness me! That's my grandfather. Thanks, Sally."

How distinguished he looked in his tweeds, standing amidst the olive green institutional drabness of Rowley Street Secondary.

"There you are, dear girl!" he kissed her on the cheek.

"What are you doing here, Grandpa? Nothing's wrong, I hope?"

"No, no, Gill. I just haven't seen you for a while and I was in town, so I thought I'd drop in. Your mother told me about your move. Are you comfortable. Everything all right?"

"I'm fine, Grandpa, thanks. It's great to see you!"

He took her hand and squeezed it. "Any chance of a wee chat? Could I take you somewhere? It's a bit late for afternoon tea."

Dare she risk it? Why not? She had nothing to hide. It would certainly be a fascinating confrontation! "As a matter of fact, Grandpa, I usually see a friend about this time."

"Willie?"

"Well, yes."

"I'd like to meet him, Gill. Really."

"All right. I suppose you know something about him from Mum and Dad?"

"They've given me an idea, but I'd like to form my own opinion."

"Give me a minute to clear up and I'll be with you Grandpa. Willie will be in a fairly grotty old pub along the road. D'you mind?"

Hector Colquhoun grinned. "I've been in some fairly grotty spots in my time, Gill."

When they entered the Argyle Willie detached himself from Lex, Mo and Tommy Bell. Gill introduced him to her grandfather.

"Very glad to meet you, Willie. I hear you're shaking up our dozy Scottish Establishment! About time."

Willie was momentarily nonplussed by this conversational thrust, quite unexpected from a figure at least outwardly so obviously Establishment himself.

"Aye, yes, I do what I can to keep issues up front, as you might say."

"And no doubt get up sundry noses in the process?"

"Uh-huh. Inevitable." Willie smiled uncertainly. "Can I get you a drink? Gill, we could sit over yonder."

"Thank you. A bottle of light ale will be fine. I've left my landrover up near Renfrew Street. It's a fair way back to Fintry too."

"Just a bitter lemon for me, Willie," said Gill, guiding the Major to the vacant table. She was aware of the covert curiosity of Lex and the other two.

When they were settled Willie tried a polite gambit. "So you were regular in the army, Major Colquhoun?"

"I joined the TA just before the War. I suppose I considered it as a career, but by 1946 I'd had enough, so I quit and went into business. Broking. I stayed with the Territorials though, until they kicked me out in '68."

"Was it Artillery or what?"

"No, the good old Highland Light Infantry, till they amalgamated with the Scots Fusiliers anyway. 1959 that was." He raised his glass. "Here's health to you both." Since neither said anything after this toast, the Major said, "You'd be too young for National Service, Willie?"

"Yes, thank goodness. By many years."

"Ah well, I believe those two years in the Forces did most young men a power of good. However, it's a stage long past." He calculated, then asked, "What about your father, Willie. He'd have been of an age for National Service?"

Gill noticed a certain uneasiness in Willie's face.

"Yeah, he was."

"Army?" persisted the Major.

"HLI, actually."

"*Really*? Well then, perhaps I knew him in the TA. Devine? What was his rank?"

"You wouldn't have known him, Major."

"I might have."

"His first name was Patrick, wasn't it, Willie?," Gill put in, she hoped helpfully.

Willie closed his eyes and passed a hand resignedly over his hair. "He spent most of his time in custody, the glasshouse, till he got a dishonourable discharge. See, he was a Communist from way back and just wouldn't take the discipline."

The Major put his head on one side and raised his eyebrows. "The Russians were our allies in the War."

"Not during the Cold War. Anyhow, he was screwed up from the start. Hungry, you know. Pinching things with the other boys. Wee things like apples and sweeties."

"Mmm," said the Major.

"So of course he got roughed up by the police. Then it was the juvenile courts and the birch. Several go's he had. After the army it was drink. Frankly he'd been a wino in the making since about fourteen. And his father too. He came over from Donegal in the twenties. Unemployed most of his life."

"Dear, dear. Is your father still alive, Willie?"

"Died 1974. I was fifteen."

"Brothers, sisters?"

"Gill knows the story, don't you Gill?"

"Two brothers, two sisters, isn't it Willie?"

"Right, but I don't see much of any of them. Not since my mother moved out to Drumchapel. They've all married and disappeared into the woodwork, if you know what I mean."

The other two nodded. "I think you're the bright one, Willie. Your mother must be proud of you."

"Well, let's say, Major, I'm the only one who seems to see any point in making an effort. My mother's not *that* pleased. She's really an old Churchill Tory if she'd admit it!"

The Major allowed himself to be persuaded to take another bottle of beer, providing he paid for the round.

"I can't say I read the *Glasgow Recorder*, Willie, but I've been shown some of your pieces. You certainly lay it on strong about the Tory majority's being uninterested in Scottish affairs."

"Somebody has to speak out."

"I agree with you there. I don't like a good deal of what I see today. English ways. Armed Services cutbacks to say nothing of youth hooliganism and downright immorality. Drugs, knives on the housing schemes. Terrible."

"The Tories can't be blamed for all that, but there's no doubt the Westminster set-up has to take a lot of responsibility. The Scots are not masters in their own house."

"You think Labour could do better?"

"Willie always insists he writes as a free agent. No party affiliation, Grandpa," said Gill.

"Well, of course I belong to our journalists' Trade Union. But what Scotland needs before anything serious can be done about her problems is a massive co-operative effort. Party politics is a luxury for later."

"I follow," said the Major, staring intently at the man opposite him. "Devolution. But Labour have promised that, haven't they?"

"Yes," said Willie, "But that's not enough."

"You don't mean independence. A complete break with the UK?"

"'Independence' is an elusive word, Major."

"Yes, but surely you'd advocate a continuing defence policy throughout the UK? Common weapons, training programmes etcetera. With an overall *British* High Command to coordinate everything."

"No, I would not," said Willie flatly.

"Good God!" Major Colquhoun was shaken.

"The nuclear threat's gone, so Scotland can save *hundreds of millions of pounds* by withdrawing from the Tories', and Labour's, Trident Nuclear Submarine Programme alone. As full independent members of the European Community, our defence arrangements should be much more EC-orientated. Mind you, we should also keep all our conventional troops in Scotland operative."

The Major shook his head vigorously. "Those Continentals? The French, the Italians, the Germans? I wouldn't trust those beggars with yesterday's newspaper."

Gill was becoming anxious but Willie laughed.

"I understand you, Major Colquhoun, but somehow we have to co-operate. Don't you think so? Or are you a Euro-sceptic?"

"No, I'm not that. The War's long over. I'm all for demolishing trade barriers and working with Europe to help our industry expand. But what you suggest, Willie, on defence – I'd have to draw the line at that."

"See, the generation looking to negotiate these matters, whether in Scotland or Europe, didn't go through the War. They don't maybe have the hangups from those days."

The Major glanced at his watch. "Which might be another way of saying, Willie, that they lack realistic experience of the risks of relaxing military vigilance. Look, I have to go. I've enjoyed talking to you. Very much. I hope we'll meet again, soon." He smiled winningly, stood up and grasped Willie's hand in a friendly gesture.

Gill rose. "Can I help you find a taxi, Grandpa?"

"No thanks. The Subway's fine. I rather enjoy it. Goodbye now, both of you." He kissed his granddaughter and left.

Willie went to the lavatory. He spoke to Lex Grant en route.

"How're y'doing, Lex?"

"O K. Who's the bloody Colonel Blimp?"

"Gill's grandfather. Nice old guy. No mug either."

"Oh aye? Is that so, Willie? Play yer fuckin' cairds right an' mebbe ye'll get tae polish his Sam Browne belt. Eh, Tommy?" He guffawed.

"You can stick that sort of fuckin' childish patter up yer arse, Lex, or maybe I'll do it for you!"

"Awright, awright, Mr Devine. Keep yer hair on, fur Chrisake. Only jokin'."

Not the first time Willie was forced to recognize how frequently his friend's clear-brained address to life was hopelessly clouded by an unreasoning, raging class envy.

Gill watched Willie coming back. How *had* she become involved with such a man? At times he was so close as to seem an inseparable, precious part of her, at others he was utterly foreign, alien almost. But none of it mattered: she loved him, she loved him. Gill was seized by a sudden warm sexual lust for Willie, to have him naked in bed with her, to feel his hard eager response to her touch. Should she ask him to go back with her to Rubyvale Street straight away?

Walter the barman called him before he reached her. They conferred briefly, then Willie gestured to her that he'd be just a minute and stepped out of the main door. Sure enough, he was back in seconds.

"What was all that about, Willie?"

"Nothing. Just someone wanting a word."

"Who?"

"Danny Ramage. Remember he came up that Saturday I had been with the plods?"

"Yes, Willie, I remember."

Gill's hungry impulse of moments ago died. An increasingly familiar anxiety took its place.

## SIX

BY NOW WILLIE DEVINE was becoming well known nationally. He appeared on a TV panel and clearly impressed the studio audience with his forthright views about the urgent need for Scottish governmental autonomy. Sales of the *Glasgow Recorder* showed a significant increase and Willie's end year remuneration package reflected this. His published comments, when they concerned Scotland's political status, continued to hold a skilful balance between predictions of peaceful progress towards constitutional change and warnings of civil tension if this were to be denied.

It was not only the Glasgow police who were keeping an eye on Willie.

The phone rang on his desk at the office. "Willie Devine? Oh hello, sir. This is Hazel Murdoch at the Scottish Labour Party's central office."

"Yes?"

"Would you be free to meet two of our senior people next Tuesday evening, sir?"

"I might, but who are they? What about?"

"The subject for discussion I don't know, Mr Devine, but I can say that both representatives are very senior. The meeting would be absolutely confidential, sir."

Willie rolled a cigarette, cradling the receiver against his shoulder. "Well, eh, I ..."

"It would be convenient and much appreciated if you could indicate your willingness now, Mr Devine. The men who wish to see you are extremely busy. Now if you ..."

"So am I, girl! Don't rush me."

"Sorry, sir. Yes, of course you have a tight schedule too. I do beg your pardon."

"'S'all right."

"So, may I say you're agreeable to the meeting on Tuesday?"

Willie wasn't sure. He didn't like being crowded. His independence was his trump card. But, he had to keep in touch with all sides and this could be a valuable opportunity to get up to the minute on Labour's inside track about the Home Rule/Devolution/Independence question. For he didn't doubt that something in that connection was what was going to be on the table.

"Aye, OK then, Hazel."

"Fine, Mr Devine. If you'll ask for Suite Number Six at the Central Hotel on Tuesday evening about seven? Is that all right?"

"Yes. I'll be there."

"Our representatives will look forward to meeting you, Mr Devine. And thank you for your time this morning."

My God! thought Willie, the Labour Party's come a long way since the days of Maxton and John McLean.

He kept the appointment to himself. Gill could be told about it afterwards, depending on what eventuated.

Willie freshened up at the Central before taking the lift up to Suite Six. He knocked and was immediately admitted.

"Willie! Come in. Nice to meet you. I'm Joe Murray, STUC. Great you could come, Willie." This broadly smiling individual pumped Willie's arm, then clapped him on the back. There was a Union badge in his lapel. "Let me get you a drink. There's a wee bar over here. No heavy beer though, Willie!" he laughed genially.

The meeting suite was composed of two connected rooms. From the back room another figure now emerged. Willie immediately recognized the stocky politician, well dressed, in his late fifties: it was Jimmie Anderson MP, the party's chief spokesman in Scotland on constitutional matters.

"You made it then, Willie? Jimmie Anderson – glad to make your acquaintance." They shook hands. "Joe getting you a drink?

Whisky is it? Great, great!"

They sat, glasses in hand, in deep armchairs, and it was soon obvious that Murray's function was to keep the drinks topped up, to open packets of nuts and to empty the ashtray on the coffee table. All three smoked continuously and the room was soon filled with an eye-stinging fug. It was too cold to open a window.

"Thanks for coming up the night, Willie. We know you're a busy journalist," Anderson began.

"That's OK," said Willie noncommittally.

"There's many in high places admire your *Recorder* column, Willie, including yours truly, I may say."

"Thanks," said Willie.

Anderson laughed briefly. "You've fairly been roasting the Tories recently!" Willie did not respond. Anderson continued, "Mind you, we're not always sure which side of the fence you're on. That no right, Joe?"

"Uh-huh. That's right, Jimmie."

"See, obviously in our book, in the Party like, we consider that if you're not for the Conservatives then Labour's the only alternative. Especially in Scotland. What d'you say, Willie?"

"I know what you mean, Jimmie," he replied. "On a lot of issues. But I'm mainly concerned with Scotland's constitutional status."

"So are we, Willie, so are we. As a matter of fact that's my particular field too."

Willie looked him in the eye. "I'm aware of *that*."

"Aye, well, I'd like to dwell on that area for a wee while. OK?"

"Fine."

"Let me make it clear, Willie, in these walls, that what I have to say is coming with the approval of the very top. Know what I mean?"

"That's definitely right. From the very top," echoed Murray.

"I understand," said Willie.

"Well now, we've been noticing a new, what you might call a strident new tone in your articles. And let me say again, Willie, you're much admired. It's just that sometimes what you say isn't

88

that supportive of Labour policy. Know what I mean?"

"No I don't." Willie was sitting up very straight. "Neither the *Glasgow Recorder* nor I is a mouthpiece for *any* Party."

Jimmie Anderson gently indicated to Joe Murray that he should fill their glasses. He offered Willie a cigarette.

"No thanks. I prefer my roll-ups."

Anderson smiled thinly. "I used to smoke those when I was on the railways." He lit his own. "Don't get me wrong, Willie. We respect the Press's independence."

"Well?"

"Let's look at it this way. We think we have the right policies for Scotland's future, *including* a Parliament in Edinburgh. We believe our policies are truly patriotic and, once we're in power, once the ruddy Tories have been kicked into oblivion, we'll not delay in implementing those policies. It'll all be laid out again in our next manifesto." He took his recharged glass and drank slowly, letting his words sink in. "Now you, Willie, we're sure that you are likewise a true Scottish patriot. But sometimes, just sometimes, we don't seem to be rowing in the same boat."

"It's not hard to explain. You are ..."

Anderson raised an imperious hand. "Hear me out, Willie. Then we'll listen to what you've got to say. Now then, just to recap, we've got the Labour Party committed to a devolved Scottish Parliament and we've got Willie Devine with a powerful, respected voice in a Scottish mass circulation paper. Right? We in the Party need all the support we can get to make sure of an overwhelming mandate at the next election to bring in constitutional reform. Are you reading me, Willie?"

"Loud and clear. But I don't think your proposed policies go far enough, you see. What's needed ..."

"Hold on, laddie!" said Anderson, "You're still no with me. Let me spell it out more clearly. But, look, I'm peckish, aren't you?"

"It doesn't matter."

"Och, we might as well be comfortable. Joe, ring room service on the phone through there. Order an ashet of sandwiches. Smoked salmon and turkey. OK? And three bottles of chilled white wine. Chablis if they've got it." Joe complied. "Now Willie, let's see if we can get at this business. We're both for change in Scotland's political situation. Right? Aye. Now there's a difference on the perceived best way of securing that change. Are you with me so far, Willie?"

"Yes, Jimmie, I'm with you, but it's that difference that's the bother." Anderson again made to cut him short but Willie insisted on continuing this time. "Labour's promise to the electorate, however it's dressed up, is for Devolution, a devolved Scottish Parliament, with limited powers. I do not think that will solve our problems, for various reasons, and I can't see a way to bridge that difference."

"Well, I think you'd better, boy."

"Is that some kind of threat, Jimmie?"

"Not at all, not at all, Willie. What I'm saying, and remember I told you this is from the top, is that we should be *co-operating*, not nit-picking, *unproductively*, on these issues."

"Meaning what exactly?"

"Well, look, Labour's got a real chance of getting in, with a strong majority for once, at the next election. The polls say so. But we're no counting our chickens, Willie. Know what I mean? We want to do all we can to make bloody certain o' it. And if we're to carry out our policies in Scotland ... well, what I'm saying, Willie, is that a man like yourself can exert *influence*, great influence on the Scottish voters."

"So I should peddle the Labour Party's line?"

"Willie, who else is going to do any good? The Tories don't figure here at all. The Nationalists will never get more than a minority vote, a protest vote."

Willie took his time before saying, "Jimmie, did it ever occur to you that your big vote in Scotland in recent years might not be anything more than a protest vote?"

The MP's reply surprised Willie. "Oh yes. We're quite aware of that. That's why we're determined to squash the SNP. They musn't be allowed to get up a head of steam."

"I can see the logic of that," said Willie, "But the fact is your party's policy is to maintain the Westminster structure, isn't it?"

The sandwiches and wine arrived. While the steward was opening the bottles, then getting Joe Murray's signature on the chits, Anderson said, "We'll pick this up in a minute, Willie. Time we made some progress." He was already eating greedily.

When they were alone again Willie quickly said, "Jimmie, I think we're heading into a blind alley."

"Just bide a wee, Willie lad," said Anderson with an elaborate show of patience. "I've more to say to you. But eat! Joe, pour the wine."

They munched. Murray remarked, "Always nice and fresh, the Central's sandwiches." Clearly Suite Six was a frequent venue for the two politicians.

"I want to lay our cards on the table, Willie," said Anderson, recommencing negotiations. "Face up, like. We think you could be of great assistance to the Labour effort towards the next General Election, if you were minded to help. Who knows how we might co-operate in the future?"

"Just what is that supposed to mean, Jimmie?"

The older man looked about in an instinctive gesture. "What I'm saying, Willie, is that if your column – you ken, what you write in your *Recorder* articles over the next few months – if you were to take more of a socialist line, well, I mean ..."

Willie cut in: "Spell it out, Jimmie."

"Aye, right. What we think you should be doing is *backing* the Devolution option and that. Understand? Cut out the bloody SNP stuff. That way we could all work together, Willie. Long term." Anderson looked up, smiling. "For Scotland's sake, Willie."

"Long term? How's that?"

Murray got up. "I'll take a walk next door, Jimmie. There's a game on the telly. OK?"

"OK, Joe." Anderson took a mouthful of wine. "We'd really like to harness your talents, Willie. Now, listen. Paddy Meffen's our Press Secretary. Plus PR. Well, Paddy's due for retirement next year. High profile job, Willie, without the bloody deadlines. Eh?"

"Go on," said Willie quietly.

Anderson smiled again. "'Course, we realize you may have personal political ambitions. With your reputation and Union membership you could be a first class candidate for us."

"With a flat in London maybe?"

The MP's face was impassive. He sensed the possibility of another mission about to be successfully accomplished. "It's a great life down there, you know." He caught himself. "But *you'd* want to take your place in the Scottish Assembly, wouldn't you, Willie? Whichever, you'd be in the driving seat with us. And if I read it right we could be in for a bloody long time, my friend. The Tories have had a hell of a run. Now it's our turn for a ride on the gravy train. What d'you say, Willie Devine?" Anderson leant back, grinning confidently.

"I say you can fuck off, Jimmie."

The already rubicund face darkened further. Murray reappeared.

"Now listen to me, son!" Anderson wagged a finger at Willie. "I wonder if you realize how delicate your position is?"

"What the hell are you talking about?"

"I'm talking police surveillance, Willie. I'm talking your bloody job, boy!"

"I'm a journalist. I say whatever I ..."

"Aw, stow that shite, man!" Anderson shouted, bending forward aggressively on the edge of his chair. "See, we know about you and your friends. We also know about a recent visit you had from the Special Branch, Willie. Oh aye, there's plenty just waiting for you to put a foot wrong. I advise you to change your tune pretty soon. Look ... we know the *Recorder* folks. Old friends, like." He wagged his finger again. "Just you bear that well in mind, Willie."

Could he say anything to pacify this ugly bugger? How was he going to extricate himself with the most effective limitation of potential damage? Willie could see no way out. He decided simply to speak the truth. "Jimmie, I think you underestimate the value papers like the *Recorder* place on their editorial freedom. Unless they genuinely believe in a party's policies they're not going to back them. My view, which the *Recorder* has endorsed for a while now, is that the Devolution your party is offering the Scottish people will not fill the bill, even if you are sincere, which not everyone accepts anyway. We have to throw off completely the dead hand of the 1707 Treaty of Union if the Scots are to govern themselves sensibly, if we're to recover our national identity, our self-respect as an independent member of the EC. That's my opinion and I can't alter it, Jimmie."

Anderson was on his feet. "Ach, Devine! You'd better piss off. You must be deaf – you've obviously no heard one fuckin' word I've said." He gestured with his head. "Beat it." Then he added, "Oh, eh, don't get any smart aleck ideas about reporting this meeting. It was confidential."

The obsequious Murray nodded. "I didnae hear a thing, Jimmie. I was in the other room watching telly the whole time."

Anderson's lip curled, revealing yellow tobacco-stained teeth. "All I can remember, Willie, is that you were asking about the chances of a flat in London. By God! You'd better watch your step." He waved his arms about. "Aw, just get out my fuckin' sight!"

Joe Murray already had the door open.


On his way back to Rubyvale Street Willie was seething with an uncertain anger. He felt soiled. But was he being naïve? Politics was the art of the possible. It always would be, in a democracy. Was he being unrealistic in imagining great, early change in Scotland? Would the people rise to it, ever? Or were they so lethargic and uninterested that they were content to let the Jimmie Andersons of this world control their destiny? Were they prepared to sink further into the status of provincial backwater where nothing of importance happened except by courtesy of a group of policy-makers hundreds of miles outside the country? For that was what Labour's Devolution still meant at the end of the day.

Willie knew that he didn't lack courage. He'd be prepared to risk unpopularity, he was willing to put his job on the line if it came to it, even his Union membership and all that would mean for his future career. But this sudden feeling of insecurity about his deepest convictions, that was painful, debilitating, intolerable. He'd tell Gill all about it; that might help.

She was waiting for him at Rubyvale Street. He'd given her a key of her own.

"Willie darling! You looked washed out."

"I am, Gill."

"Whisky?"

"No, I've had enough of that. Tea please."

"Right. There's some sausages. Fancy them?"

"No thanks, just hot tea. I've got a very bad taste in my mouth, Gill."

"Oh?"

He sat down and stretched vigorously, his hands, fisted, extended above his head. "I've just been with Messrs. the Labour Party"'

"Who were they, Willie?"

"Doesn't matter, Gill. One politician's much the same as another."

"But were they well known? Names I'd recognize?"

"Oh yes, heid bummers right enough."

"So who were they?"

"I said it doesn't matter, sweetheart. It's what they say that counts."

Gill made a face. She was annoyed. "I have to say, Willie, I don't appreciate this always being kept at arm's length. Surely by now I've got some right to be told what's going on in your life, your job?"

He shook his head from side to side as if to say that he regretted it but did not intend changing his stand. "If those buggers meant what they said maybe I won't *have* a job much longer."

"*What*?" Gill was shocked.

He explained the thinly veiled threat.

"That's terrible, Willie. Not fair. Don't they respect the freedom of the press? They are Democrats, aren't they?"

"Oh aye, they're Democrats. But they're also determined to win the next election."

Gill pondered for a moment. "Couldn't you have agreed to accommodate them? I mean, just to an extent?"

"Not without compromising my own views, which can't really be reconciled with their Devolution policy. You know that, Gill."

"Yes, but you could give some space to outlining their case. You wouldn't necessarily have to say you agreed with it."

"That was *not* what they were after."

Gill frowned. "Did they imagine they could simply persuade you to take their line? They must have realized you wouldn't just change like that. Not for a few whiskies ... and no doubt a bit of flattery?"

"They had other inducements up their sleeve."

"Such as, Willie? Or am I not to be told in case I rush out into the street and shout about it?" There was slightly more colour than usual in Gill's cheeks.

Willie massaged his forehead in a gesture of tiredness. "There's a nice upcoming spot as the Party's Press and PR man in Scotland. Mind you, I reckon they would genuinely like me in that position."

"I see."

"Or, if I happened to be interested, they could probably get me selected as a candidate."

Gill's eyes widened. "You mean ... for Parliament? To be an MP? God, Willie! What did you say to that?"

"What d'you think? Told them to fuck off."

"Why on earth? Couldn't you at least have said you'd consider the matter? I mean ..." She was now agitated.

"Gill, Gill, of course I couldn't do that. There's no way I ..."

She shouted, "So you came away having turned down a lifetime opportunity to get into Parliament, where you might actually be able to *do* something about Scotland's problems. And you antagonize powerful people who can smash you, who can make sure you lose your job so you can do absolutely *nothing* for bloody Scotland! Funny logic, Willie Devine!"

He moved to put his arm round her. "Listen, I ..."

"Don't touch me!" She stood up.

"I think you're confused about the issue here, Gill."

She shouted again, "I'm *not* confused. But obviously it's utterly irrelevant what I think. I'm not to be told a thing about what goes on, but I'm still expected to swing along with Willie Devine. Well, I'm not a doormat! I refuse to be treated like one. I've gone to bed with you. I've allowed you to alienate my family. For what? Political theories that are probably impractical? Maybe I've been an idiot. And what happens if you get kicked off the *Recorder*? My teacher's salary isn't that great, you know."

"You bitch!" It was Willie's turn to shout now. "You're way off beam. I didn't know till this minute that you considered my political views of such little account. Thanks for making yourself clear." Gill had started to cry. "Stop snivelling. Christ! I've had enough for tonight. I'm going to the Argyle. *Don't follow me*!" He grabbed his anorak and slammed the door.

Gill sat whimpering for the next two hours. Her thoughts leapt around uncontrollably. What in God's name *did* she believe in politically? Was Willie barking up the wrong tree after all? Labour had an iron grip on Scotland's voters, didn't they? But he was hostile to them. And yet, as far as she knew, he'd not admitted to a totally SNP commitment either. Gill herself had never really doubted that the Tories, the common-sense party of business, would eventually regain a position of influence in Scottish affairs: how could she, coming from her background? It was all so horribly confusing.

She was not going back to Jordanhill until she'd put matters right with Willie. She wished desperately now that she'd not shouted at him. He'd been strung up enough already without her attacking him as well. Oh Willie! As the night advanced all Gill wanted was the chance to comfort her lover, to take him to bed and enfold him in her arms.

But by two in the morning there was no sign of him. She must have slept in the chair for an hour since it had been one o'clock when she'd last looked at her watch. By three she was forced to recognize that he was not coming back that night. She left and was fortunate to pick up a taxi cruising down Byres Road.

She rang him several times next day, but to no avail. It was too daunting to go looking for him in the pub. Miserable, she repeated the process the following day. Still no Willie. The evening after that she talked Cathie into visiting the Argyle. Hamish MacCorquodale and Tommy Bell were there. The girls bought drinks and joined them.

"Ah, our beautiful ladies!" said Hamish, beaming one of his charming smiles. "Chillian, what have you done with Willie Devine?"

"Not guilty, Hamish. Have you not seen him then?"

"I have not. Nor Lex Grant. But he's often away on one of his ploys. Willie's the regular. I hope he's OK."

"Why d'you say that?"

Hamish saw the anxiety in Gill's face. Instinctively he patted her hand. "No, nothing at all, at all! I've no information." He had an idea. "Are there any demonstrations on just now? Maybe he's been sent again to cover them. Tommy, are there demonstrations anywhere that you've heard of?"

"No," was the typical response from the drab individual in the donkey jacket.

Cathie and Gill soon left.

She'd promised not to phone Willie at his office, but after he'd been absent from her life for six days Gill could no longer forbear. The switchboard girl assured her that Mr Devine had been about in the course of the previous week, but was sorry that he was not presently at his desk. Would Madam call later? What was the name, please? Gill put the phone down without replying. She was distraught. Did Willie never want to see her again?

He rang her the same day just as she was packing up after school and asked her to come to Rubyvale Street. They fell on one another, hugging hotly, both apologizing simultaneously between passionate kisses. They even laughed at themselves.

"Oh, Willie! Where have you been? I was nearly dead worrying. I thought you'd done with me. I ..."

"My dear wee Gill, you'll not get rid of me that easily. I love you – remember?"

Gill was weeping, just a bit, with relief. "Me too, Willie Devine. More than I knew." She wiped her eyes with her handkerchief. "Nevertheless, I want to know where you've been hiding."

"Lex Grant's place."

"Of course."

"I felt we needed a cooling-off period, so I kept a low profile, and stayed out of the Argyle too."

"All I care about is we're together again. Listen, Willie, about our argument ... I mean, the political points, well ..."

"Forget it, Gill. We don't need to go into all that again. Not now anyhow."

"No, Willie, I've done a lot of thinking the past few days. I see now why you reacted as you did at that meeting with those Labour people. You couldn't have done otherwise."

"That's all right then."

"Yes, and Willie?"

"Uh-huh?"

"I admire you very very much."

He grinned. "I consider that one hell of a come-on! So come here this minute while I get your clothes off, my beauty."

Happily Gill yielded to his eager hands. Soon they were on the bed, coupled in mutual abandonment to a surging, thrusting orgasmic frenzy.

In ecstasy Gill cried out, "Willie darling! Never never leave me, will you?"

"Never," he said, gusts of his breath coming in her face.


Willie hadn't long to wait for a development from the abortive Central Hotel meeting. A confidential memorandum appeared on his desk requesting his presence in the Editor's office that afternoon at three thirty. Willie found another man with Sandy Black when he opened the Editor's door.

"Come in, Willie!" said Black cheerfully. "This is Mr Graham Harbottle, an owners' representative. Graham, Willie Devine."

"How do, Willie." The accent was North Country. They shook hands.

"You on the Board, Graham?"

"Aye, but only non-executive. I try to help when I can."

"I see." A picture was forming in Willie's mind.

Black's secretary brought in a tray of tea and biscuits. "Shall I pour, Mr Black?"

"No, it's all right, May. I'll play Mum." She left and he filled the cups. "Help yourselves to milk and sugar. Biscuit, Graham?"

When they were settled again Harbottle said, "Willie, we're all pleased on the Board with your contribution to the *Glasgow Recorder*'s current reputation for outspokenness. I've read a good many of your articles. Fine work."

"Thanks very much, Graham."

Black spoke: "And you know I endorse that, Willie. One hundred and one percent."

"I trust your remuneration and other conditions are fully satisfactory?" Harbottle enquired.

"I'm not complaining," Willie replied.

"Good, good," said the proprietors' man, smiling. "We wouldn't like to lose you."

"Poached, you mean? No, I'm happy enough here, Graham, if that's what's maybe on your mind."

"I didn't mean it quite that way, Willie."

"What exactly ... ?"

Black spoke again: "I think I'd be right in saying that Graham was being purely hypothetical, Willie. Personally I can't really envisage circumstances in which the *Recorder* would want to dispense with your services."

Suddenly Willie knew what this conference was about. His heart started to hammer. "Go on, Sandy," he said.

"Well, Willie, you and I have talked about your material before, haven't we?"

"I remember, yes."

Black looked at Harbottle. "Graham, would you like to take it from there?"

"Righto, Sandy," said the rather ponderous Harbottle, putting down his cup and saucer. "I like to call a spade a spade, Willie, so I'll come straight to the point. This newspaper has been in business for a long time and it's proud of its independent editorial line. Nevertheless, over the years some solid alliances have been forged, politically you understand? Let's say to the left of centre, Willie. That's our constituency and that's where we sell our newspapers. Am I making myself clear?"

"Oh yes, quite clear, Graham."

"Well then, what I have to say to you is this, Willie. Up here in Bonnie Scotland you have a few local problems concerning Local government and the Westminster Parliament's correct relationship with a possible future Edinburgh Assembly. Am I right? I mean, that is the area which particularly interests you, isn't it?"

Sandy Black was nodding solemnly, his eyes for the moment conveniently closed. Willie said merely, "Yes, that's accurate."

"Now then, Willie," Harbottle continued, "you've written some pretty scalding pieces recently. Even upset the coppers, I hear!" He laughed. "That never bothered us. Good publicity. But we've got to be careful not to be too partisan, you know. Even-handedness should always be the watchword, Willie, don't you agree?"

"What are you driving at, Graham?"

Harbottle removed his spectacles, quickly polished the lenses with his breast pocket silk handkerchief and replaced them. "What I'm saying is that our friends on the left, influential friends, Willie, might feel that the *Recorder* was becoming hostile to *their* ideas of what's best for Scotland. As I've already said, there's room for debate in your column, Willie."

"As long as it isn't antithetical to the policy of the Labour Party. That's it, isn't it, Graham?"

"You're being a bit black and white, Willie," said Black.

"Sandy," said Harbottle, "I believe this clever reporter of yours understands us. I think we should ask him to dwell on the matter privately, and leave it at that for now. What d'you say, Willie?"

"Well, I've heard you. And there are a few issues other than the Government of Scotland to write about as well." He managed a grin.

"Ataboy!" said Graham Harbottle. When Willie had gone he told Black that he was pleased with the success of his mission.

Willie made his way straight to the Argyle.

"Lex, I'm glad you're here. Where's Mo?"

"Some family do at the Paradise tonight."

"Good. Expecting anyone else?"

"Tommy Bell probably. But later. Why?"

Willie confided to his friend the bare details of his afternoon meeting.

"What are you going to dae, Willie?"

"Nothing. I mean, carry on as normal. That's the bloody point, Lex."

"Sorry. Spell it oot, will you? I'm no with you."

"I've no intention of toeing any bloody party's line, Lex. I'll write what I believe in. I've always done that."

"So you have, Willie, so you have."

"Well, maybe the honeymoon's over. There is pressure, political pressure, being placed on the *Recorder*'s editorial side, Lex. I'm sure of it. Christ knows what unholy deals are being made. Anyway, the thing is I've been told straight to give support in the column to the Labour line on Devolution. Otherwise ..." He drew his index finger across his throat.

"You couldnae do that, Willie."

"Precisely."

"So free speech bites the dust. Hey, Willie, could you lose you job over this?"

"Lex, you finally got there!"

"My God!" Lex Grant's brain was racing. "This is serious. I mean, we're *relying* on you to get a right message out in the Press when the balloon goes up, before the rest of the lickspittle hacks mess it all up."

"I've got the piece more or less finalized for a front page special."

Lex was now looking exceedingly anxious. "How long have we got, Willie?"

"Three or maybe four weeks. I can string things along with some harmless crap about the cost of the Royal Family, water privatisation, or turning folks out of the asylums – for a while anyway. But the first time I'm seen to be criticizing Labour again it could be the bullet."

"Right. Listen, I'll have to go. I'm needing a word with Danny Ramage. Urgent. Thanks for the pint."

## SEVEN

IN THE WAKE of Glasgow's liquid New Year celebrations there was a sudden diversion. Tommy Bell's novel won the Halliday Prize for contemporary fiction. The author's friends and acquaintances were stunned.

Walter Torrance, the barman at the Argyle, reacted typically: "Ah thought Ah kenned Tommy pretty well, but Ah hud nae idea at a' that he wis *that* fuckin' gude. 'Course Ah've no read ony o' his bukes, like. Ah'm jist pleased for Tommy and Nettie, y'know? Ah suppose it's kinna a compliment tae Glesca too."

Hamish MacCorquodale confided in Lex Grant. "It's a great thing for Tommy, Lex. That's obvious, and good for him. He'll maybe be going up in the world now, eh? Amazing, in a way."

"Whit d'ye mean 'amazing', Hamish?"

"Well, it's ... I ... have you read *Those Shining Walls*, Lex?"

"No properly. I've dipped in though."

"You'll have seen enough then. Would you yourself have picked it for a winner of the top literary award?"

"I wouldnae hiv a clue aboot that, Hamish. Some of they Halliday novels in the last year or two hiv been gey odd. I'm no concerned wi' judgin'. The fact is Tommy's won and that's great for Scotland. I mean, he's wan o' us. No some stuck-up anglicized cunt. Frankly, I couldnae care less whit the *content* o' Tommy's book is."

"Yes," said Hamish, looking suddenly pensive, "I understand what you're saying, Lex. I'm chust wondering what the critics will make of it."

Willie had read the book before the announcement. When he'd

finished it Gill had asked his opinion.

"Strange sort of work."

"What's it about, Willie?"

"Hard to say really. It's mainly this wee Glasgow man soliloquizing about his life. He's not happy with his lot and says so with regularity. There may be some symbolism in it. I don't know."

"Is it well written?"

"Again that's not easy to say, Gill. It's not like a traditional novel, that's for sure. Just largely stream of consciousness stuff."

"Joycean?"

Willie laughed. "I doubt if old James Augustine Aloysius would be too pleased with the comparison! No, it's not on that level. For a start, unless you belong to these parts you're going to have one hell of a job deciphering the text. Solid Glesca gutter."

"You mean it's inaccessible to the non-Glasgow reader? But that's bound to restrict sales, isn't it?"

"Severely, I'd guess, Gill. I honestly cannot imagine why the London publisher could have taken it on. It's jammed full of effing and blinding too."

Gill shook her head with shared incredulity.

"Do I gather you don't think much of *Those Shining Walls* then, Willie?"

"Och, look, I'm not saying it's *totally worthless*. It's just not my cup of tea and I certainly can't see it winning the Halliday in a million years. I think it's amazing it's made the shortlist. You'd better read it yourself, Gill." He handed her the hardback.

Gill read it with difficulty. She saw no reason to differ from Willie's conclusions.

On the day of the televised result Tommy Bell was in London for the grand occasion. The Argyle's habitués broke off their unending arguments at the bar and watched the screen open-mouthed with the writer's friends. When their hero stepped up to receive his cheque a great cheer went up. Subsequent discussion of the matter at the bar tended to centre on the £30,000 cheque: it was astonishing how many individuals were on intimate terms with Tommy Bell.

The main celebration in the Argyle was fixed for two evenings later when Bell would be back. Seven p.m. was the appointed hour, but a flushed and uncharacteristically cheerful Bell failed to arrive until nearer nine. By then his drouthy companions had already celebrated the triumph thoroughly. Most had speed-read 'Walls' since the announcement.

"What did you think of it, Lex?" asked MacCorquodale. "Now that you've read it properly." Hamish's glasses were slightly askew.

"Terrific! Fuckin' fantastic!"

"Indeed, there was a lot of fantasy."

"I dinnae mean that lit ... lit ... literally, Hamish. I'm jist sayin' it's fantastically *gude*."

"Yes, yes, I see, Lex. That's your view. What d'you feel about it, Cathie?"

Cathie Lonie, who'd come along with Gill, looked uncomfortable. "It's certainly different. But poetry's more my thing. Ask Gill."

"What does the beautiful Chill say?" Hamish made a small gesture of deference.

"I find most modern fiction difficult," she responded. "Willie and I agree that Tommy's caught the dialect brilliantly, although I'm not sure he needed so many swear words. Also, the narrative ..."

Lex interrupted, "If you want tae get the local patter right you cannae jist leave out the words you dinnae happen to like." He hiccupped.

Willie spoke: "It's a matter of the quantity, Lex. You can get the same effect with just the occasional strong language. Not necessary to lay it on too thick."

"I have to say that that's my view too," said MacCorquodale. "But obviously the Halliday judges weren't bothered."

Mo Hossein had been sitting quietly, his head flicking from one speaker to another. He now said, "Those judges are looking to the *underlying* story, not the rough language of Jock Thomson, the central character."

Lex regarded the normally silent Mo through slightly bloodshot eyes. "So what's the story, Mo?"

"Oh, eh ... it's, you know, autobiographical. Jock's career in charge of Gents toilets in Glasgow."

"You found it interesting, Mo?" asked Willie.

"Oh yes, *very* interesting. Very well written." He stood up. "Can I get new drinks? Hamish?" Mo clearly did not wish to be questioned further.

MacCorquodale pointed at Willie to gain his attention. "What did you make of the historical references? Prince Charlie, Mary Queen of Scots, Robert Louis Stevenson, and so on? Pretty weird line up, Willie, wasn't it? Making them all contemporary at least?"

Lex answered. "The *Scots Gazette* thought that aspect was fuckin' brilliant. I've got all the bloody reviews here." He pulled out of his camouflage jacket pocket a fistful of newspaper cuttings. "Wait'll I find the *Gazette* bit. Aye, here it is. Listen to this."

But at that moment a grinning Tommy Bell came into the pub. There was a commotion as all and sundry tried to shake his hand and offer congratulations. He raised his two hands, palms outwards, to fend off his well-wishers, then gave Walter two fifty pound notes, telling him to offer drinks all round, before slumping down exhaustedly in the bosom of his friends.

"Whaur's Nettie?" asked Lex.

"Sleepin' off a party the neighbours gied us at dinner time. Christ, I'm fair buggered! Sorry I'm late."

"No at a', Tommy. No at a'," said Lex, projecting maximum sympathy. "Hey, you're gettin' a helluva gude press for 'Walls'! Are ye no?"

"Uh-huh. The Scottish papers in particular."

"That's understandable now, Tommy, I'd say. The English bouquets will come later."

"Aye, maybe, Hamish. We'll see."

"There have been some reports elsewhere," said Cathie.

Once a large measure of Black Label whisky and a pint of Youngers heavy beer had been put in front of Tommy, Lex unfolded the *Scots Gazette* article. "Let me read this out," he said. "Doesnae matter if some of you hiv seen it a'ready. The headline is 'Glasgow

Author Wins Halliday: Brilliant Fantasy Novel'. Then the review, at least the bits that matter. I've marked them. Right:

> Tommy Bell's new novel, entitled THOSE SHINING WALLS, is a funny, sad, penetrating psychological study of great insight into an ordinary man's inner life. Jock Thomson is an attendant in Glasgow Central Station's Gentlemen's Lavatory. Although a lowly individual of no great intellect, Jock is not defeated by life. He takes great pride in the cleanliness of his white-tiled domain – hence the title – and he dreams. How he dreams! Bonnie Prince Charlie, Walter Scott, Robert the Bruce, William Wallace, even Mary Queen of Scots (in drag, naturally) are all users of Jock's urinals. He talks to them and tells them where they went wrong in their affairs: in turn they give him advice as to how he should conduct his own declining years. This is high farce, Tommy Bell at fantastical full stretch ... THOSE SHINING WALLS is a thoroughly modern multi-layered narrative, but it derives from an ancient and peculiarly Scottish genre of ghaistly glamourie, tales of the supranatural told on dark nights by the shennachie. Some critics may find Bell's earthy language not to their taste – e.g. the West of Scotland dialect word 'shite' appears over 1,000 times in the text – but the Halliday judges are to be commended for not allowing this courageous linguistic integrity to deter them."

"That's marvellous, Tommy," said MacCorquodale with enthusiasm. "Nice touch about the shennachie."

Lex was ready with another report. "This is the *Glasgow*

*Standard* or hiv you a' seen it? Came oot yesterday morn." Several had missed it. "OK. Here goes:

### GLASGOW WRITER TAKES TOP LITERARY PRIZE

Tommy Bell has won the Halliday Award with his novel, THOSE SHINING WALLS, a great tribute to the renaissance in Scottish fiction writing in recent years. 'Walls' is a gritty mixture of historical fantasy and the down to earth realism of Jock Thomson's life today as an underground lavatory supervisor in Glasgow's Central Station. Poor Jock has had little education and feels himself excluded from the throbbing activity above him of hurrying passengers and busy railway employees. He takes refuge in fantasy, chatting with a succession of Scottish historical figures from Saint Columba to Prince Charles Edward Stuart to Robert Louis Stevenson. Jock tells them what he thinks of them and these august personages reply with helpful advice. This is sometimes very funny, perhaps particularly so when Mary Queen of Scots arranges to come down to Jock's little office in male attire. From there she gets her kicks spying on the likes of Robert the Bruce, Andrew Carnegie and Rab Burns making use of the urinal ... This is an outstandingly original work, not least in the uninhibited use of low-life language: the employment of the expressive 'shite' 1,231 times, is a case in point. The publishers are to be congratulated on their courage, as is Tommy Bell. Glasgow and all Scotland can celebrate a richly merited, and perhaps overdue, reward to one of the English-speaking world's finest writers working today in the field of fiction."

Willie smiled benignly. "Can't ask for more than that, Tommy. Well done. There was a mention in the *Recorder* too, but it's a different department from mine of course. The book reviewers are outside, freelance usually."

"Here, I've got the *Recorder* cuttin', Willie," said Lex. "Let's see ... aye,

> 'There's going to be a hooley down Partick way soon! Tommy Bell, a long-time resident of said district, has just won the Halliday Award for his uproarious novel, set in Jock Thomson's Central Station Toilet, THOSE SHINING WALLS. Jock's angry with his deal in life and vents his feelings on a collection of imagined Scottish heroes – Prince Charlie, Robert the Bruce, Keir Hardie, Bobbie Burns and others – all down for a slash against Jock's immaculate white tiles. The joke is that Mary Queen of Scots, disguised in drag, is keeking at the men from Jock's office. A good laugh. But, guys, don't give this book to your missus for her Christmas if she's sensitive to a swear or two! For instance, 'shite' figures well over 1,000 times! But maybe that's our man cocking a snook at the London literary establishment? Whatever, well done Tommy lad, well done Partick, and well done Scotland!"

Gill looked across at Willie and fleetingly put on a puzzled expression. She thought he, equally briefly, lifted his eyes heavenwards. "You're getting full coverage, Tommy. Of course you're bound to. I expect we'll see you soon on TV."

Bell was now grinning more than ever. "Tomorrow, 9.30, BBC2."

"Brilliant!" said MacCorquodale.

Lex opened another cutting. "There's a few points in the *Chronicle.*

'Searing indictment of the mindless boredom of today's underprivileged millions in post-Thacherite Britain ... bracing dialogue, laced with vivid Scottish street language ... a scream from the underdog. But the hellishness is skilfully relieved by some Grand Guignol scenes in Jock Thomson's subterranean Glasgow loo, where urinating figures such as Sir Walter Scott and Robert Burns entertain a voyeuristic Mary Queen of Scots. Meantime, Prince Charles (the bonnie one – BPC to Jock!) and Adam Smith are gloomily shooting up in the cubicles. Enigmatic symbolism here ... This reviewer has not missed (as others appear to have done) the allusion to "We're a' Jock Tamson's Bairns." THOSE SHINING WALLS is a profoundly Socialist work ...'

"Well now! I never thought of that 'Jock Tamson's Bairns'," said MacCorquodale.

Cathie was watching Tommy closely. She said, "I suppose it was intentional, that bit? The allusion?"

He hesitated, then met her eyes. "First time I've thought of it. That's the God's truth."

An uncomfortable silence greeted this.

"Aye, weel," said Lex quickly, "These reviewers are aye seein' things the writer never meant. It's the same wi' poetry. That no right, Hamish?"

"Yes, you're right enough there, Lex," replied MacCorquodale quietly. There was a glint of suspicion behind his clear-framed glasses.

New drinks were ordered, more congratulatory toasts given. Several in the company were getting quite drunk.

Lex enquired, "Is that right, Tommy, there's over 1,000 'shites'?"

"I never counted up myself," said the glassy-eyed Bell.

Lex winked at Hamish. "'Cos if that's right, whit I've got to say is that that's a helluva pile of keech, Tommy! Eh ... isn't it? ... a big load o' jobbies, Tommy! Christ!"

In attempting to illustrate his point by rounding both extended arms Lex contrived to knock over two full straight glasses of beer. Liquid promptly reached almost all their laps, trouser legs and shoes. Exclamations of annoyance and surprise brought an end to the party.

"Listen, it's late, Tommy," said Willie. "If you don't mind we'll pack it in, the girls and I."

Tommy Bell was too drunk to do more than lift a limp hand in acknowledgement. Willie helped Gill and Cathie on with their coats. Lex Grant was still speaking.

"I'm helluva sorry, Tommy. Couldnae help it. Hey, listen, aboot those 'shites' again – d'you think it's *possible* that those publisher eedjits in London took your buke *because* o' the language? Honest now."

"I don't know, Lex."

"No, I mean, that sort o' lingo's different. To their fuckin' gentle ears anyhow. I reckon they said to theirsels, 'Look here, Horace, this joker Bell's got a splendid line in gutter talk – the Glasgow variety. I believe we could package and peddle this junk. *Succès de scandale* and all that, old boy! If we hype it right, the dumb fuckin' punters will go for it, mark my word, old chap'."

Bell stared at him, his mouth open. "Christ, I just don't know, Lex."

Hamish MacCorquodale and Mo Hossein maintained silence.

As they walked along Dumbarton Road Gill remarked, "You didn't say much tonight, Willie."

"No, I thought it'd be better if I kept quiet."

The forthright Cathie craned round Gill. "Don't you agree with all those critics then, Willie? They seemed to *love* it."

"No. 'Fraid not. But those were the Scottish papers. You'd have to expect them to praise the local boy. It's understandable, up to a point. The *Chronicle* tried to make something political out of it. Bloody ridiculous."

"But the judges presumably had no particular Scottish sympathies? Not all of them anyway," said Gill.

"Och, those Halliday judges are notorious. Quixotic decisions. Some of their choices in the past have been crazy. As much for the quality of the novels they've *rejected*."

"So why d'you think they chose Tommy's book?"

"God knows. Exhaustion in the committee? Compromise? Mind you, it was probably time for a token Scot. We've had feministic women writers, blacks, Commonwealth eurasians, a Jap recently. The whole thing's suspect. First class writing is not the only criterion in my opinion."

"Pretty heavy, Willie," said Cathie, "but I actually agree entirely with you. Still, at least the award is to a Scottish writer this year."

"Correction, Cathie – a Glasgow writer. I don't think they're necessarily the same thing."

"Quite, still ..."

Willie cleared his throat. "Apart from the fact that the book's completely unreadable unless you come from these parts ... well, I mean Jock down in his lavvy, Mary Queen of Scots ... the fuckin' thing's ludicrous. I don't happen to think Scotland needs this kind of publicity right now. In my opinion *Those Shining Walls* is likely to get the elbow from the sensible people in literature, be treated with contempt. Those reports Lex read out are just by journalists latching on to the bad language, the sensation of the moment, the flavour of the week. They're already on to something else. Look, I like Tommy Bell. I'm glad he's landed some solid cash and I wish him well personally. But this book of his, and the rest like it, well ... in my view they're positively *damaging* to Scotland's interests."

"But, Willie," said Gill, "Tommy would say that that's none of his business. He's not in politics."

"Yes, I know, Gill. And he's entitled to his artistic freedom of course. But that doesn't alter the fact that readers in the South, abroad, take their cue from this kind of high profile publication. Stupid it may be but, for a while anyway, we're in danger of being laughing stocks. That's at best. At worst, we appear a bunch of crazy, girning no-hopers. Either way, I have to say this fuckin' Halliday Award's a disaster. For serious thinking folks anyway. And not just in Scotland."

In subsequent days the more measured reviews of 'Walls' in the literary journals confirmed Willie's fears uncomfortably closely. 'A distasteful farrago of lavatorial rubbish' was a phrase which stuck in Gill's mind. 'Perhaps Mr Bell's publishers are hoping to make this The Year of the Excretory Expletive' intoned *The Times Review of Literature*, scathingly dismissive. 'It is hard to imagine any other motive'.


The figure walking alone ahead of him was familiar. The faded blue anorak. Surely ... yes, it *was* Gill's Willie Devine. Major Colquhoun drew his landrover in to the kerb, braked and leant across the empty passenger seat.

"That's you, isn't it, Willie?"

The pedestrian peered into the vehicle. "Oh, hello, Major."

"What a coincidence! Look, are you busy this afternoon?"

"Not really. I've filed my copy. I was just on my way home."

"Would you come out to Fintry for a bit? Some good country air?"

Willie was curious. "Aye, OK, Major. That'd be nice."

Hector Colquhoun raised a thumb. "Hop in then."

They drove westwards.

"Fine day," observed Willie.

"Oh I like this time of year. Crisp, fresh. Great for sport. As a matter of fact I've just been in to my tailor for a fitting. New shooting suit."

"Right," said Willie, looking straight ahead.

After another mile or so the Major enquired, "Handled any weapons, Willie?"

"No."

The Major nodded wordlessly. They passed by Bearsden.

"I'd intended dropping in on my daughter, Muriel, but I think we'll press on, eh?" He turned briefly and winked at Willie.

Dungearie House was a quarter of a mile off the main road, stone-built and modestly Victorian Scots baronial in style. As they crunched to a halt on the gravel forecourt a liver and white springer spaniel rushed up and pawed at the Major's door, tail thrashing wildly. Master and dog exchanged greetings and Willie was introduced.

"This is Gypsy! Down girl, down!"

Willie was not accustomed to canine ways and accepted somewhat awkwardly Gypsy's welcoming attempt to lick his face. The Major instructed her to withdraw and obedience was instant.

"Come in, Willie. How about some tea?"

"Very nice. Thanks."

A middle-aged woman wearing a floral apron materialized in the hall.

"Ah, Margaret! This is Willie Devine, a friend of my grand-daughter, Gill. Willie, Margaret Campbell, my housekeeper."

The woman had already sized up Willie. She smiled briefly. "Did I hear you're wanting some tea, Major Colquhoun?"

"That would be grand, Margaret. Damn chilly out today."

While tea was being prepared the Major took Willie to the drawing room window and pointed out the long view to the Fintry Hills. Snow on the summits shone in the brilliant sunlight. The sky was postcard blue. Rooks flickered above a stand of tall hardwoods to the right. On the well-mown lawn outside the window a mallard and his mate waddled about aimlessly.

"A bonnie sight, Willie?"

"There's a lot of empty space."

The Major laughed indulgently. "That's what usually strikes you townees about the country. Now then, here's Margaret. Right, just over here, thanks. That's splendid, Margaret. Many thanks." And before she'd withdrawn out of earshot he added, "Wonderful woman, you know, Willie. Don't know what I'd do without her."

They drank tea, ate a slice of homemade fruit tart and a piece of shortbread each. The Major enquired about Gill and about Willie's work and was assured that all was well on both counts.

"I've thought quite a lot about our chat on defence matters, Willie. And I've been reading it up a bit too."

"Uh-huh."

"With the Soviets no longer our adversaries the whole question of a nuclear deterrent looks different."

"That's right, Major."

"I mean, we can't deter maniacs in the Middle East or anywhere else if they get hold of the bomb and decide to throw some at us. If a Star Wars shield's a practical proposition, that's fair enough. But that's for the Americans, I suppose."

"It's the huge Trident expenditure we should be saving and using the funds in Scotland, and England, on dozens of urgently needed projects. We'd still keep our conventional forces in place, well equipped and trained."

"Under an independent Scottish Command?"

"Well ... yes, but obviously we'd work closely with England. A mutual defence pact maybe, although, such an arrangement would be essentially the same as Scotland would enter into with other EC countries."

"Join NATO?"

"Presumably. If it still exists in the future."

The Major took a mouthful of tea. "Changed days, Willie. Changed days."

"Not changed enough though."

"You mean politically, I take it?"

Willie nodded. "Aye, scrapping the Act of Union. What we talked about last time in the Argyle. Mind?"

"Oh yes, I remember. And you'd let the Scottish National Party lot run things. Yes?"

"I never said that, Major."

"Maybe not, but you rule out the Tories, and Labour only want to go as far as Devolution. So – QED. Or don't you approve of the SNP either?"

"They say the right things but they've no experience of actual government. Some of them are pretty vague characters, pretty young too."

"So there's no way round it, Willie?"

"Somehow the Union Treaty's fetters have got to be broken. Then we'll attend to our affairs. But right now Scottish administrators are working with one arm tied behind their backs."

Major Colquhoun thoughtfully scratched Gypsy's head as she lay obediently beside him. "Presuming we get out of the Treaty by peaceful negotiation, you'll then be stuck with an Assembly of young, vague, inexperienced politicians. Isn't that the logic of what you're saying, Willie? Not much of an outlook for poor old Scotland."

"No, not initially maybe. There could be a hell of a stramash. What can we expect if a three hundred year system is abandoned overnight, however much it's hated. Look at Russia, and they only had Communism for seventy years!"

"Come on, Willie! That's a rather odious comparison."

"Yeah, I suppose it is. Anyway, I just believe strongly in the Scottish people and their inherent good sense. After the professionals have stopped squabbling and the Assembly has settled down to the serious business of governing the country, we'll be far better off. The Civil Service is all in place already."

The Major looked directly at his guest and caught his eye. "How would the Assembly be made up, in your opinion? Solid Labour with a sprinkling of your vague young Nationalists, I suppose?"

"Who can say? I'm not so much concerned with the very first Assembly. It's what follows in the years ahead that matters. That the Scottish Parliament, not really just an Assembly, is well administered – that's what's vital."

"But the new Parliament's membership?" the Major persisted. "Are we going to emerge as a one party state? Will democracy survive?"

"Again, *I* can't give guarantees on any of that, except that there will be Proportional Representation. All I'm saying is, if the Scots get back the freedom to govern themselves I'm quite sure they'll do it at least as well as a distant, irritated group of English MPs. And our ancient nation's pride will be restored. The people will lift their heads high again."

Major Colquhoun's expression registered considerable surprise. "Good Lord, Willie! I'd no notion you were such a romantic."

"Aye well," said Willie, perhaps ruefully, "a romantic with his feet flat on the ground, I hope." He cocked his head and looked sideways at this host. "D'you realize, Major, that if and when Scotland has free democratic elections and its own parliament is established, the Tories might eventually get a look in again?"

The Major laughed delightedly. "Full circle, Willie!" He jumped up. "On that note, I'm taking you out for a walk. Blow away the old political cobwebs. Come on."

In the hall he asked Willie to wait a moment, disappeared, then came back with a spare tweed cap for Willie in one hand, a twelve bore side-by-side shotgun in the other.

Willie put on the cap. "Thanks. What's that for?"

"Rabbits. Pest round here. Come on then."

They set off across the lawn, Gypsy bounding ahead, and were soon in an exposed grassy area strewn with stones and rush tussocks. The Major broke his gun, loaded from his Barbour pocket two cartridges and placed the weapon in the crook of his right arm.

Gypsy suddenly dashed behind some rushes, barking. Out ran a rabbit. The Major had the gun in his shoulder. He fired one barrel. The animal leapt in the air and fell dead. Gypsy brought it to her master's feet. Willie stood rooted to the spot in astonishment.

The Major picked up the rabbit by the ears. "Poor little beast," he said. "Myxomatosis, Willie. Look." The emaciated animal's eyes ran with blood at the corners. "I could tell as soon as I saw him run. The skeleton is far too slack. He wouldn't have lived long." So saying, he tossed the carcase away. "The buzzards can have him."

Willie was recovering. "I suppose you're a good shot, Major?"

"Nothing special. I did reach a fair standard in the TA, but that's years ago. Like to have a go?"

"No, no. I'll just watch you, Major."

"Not good enough, Willie Devine. You might have to defend Scotland one day!"

They laughed heartily together, a rising sharp wind snatching away their voices.

Willie zipped up his anorak. "Bloody cold."

"Right. I don't want to stand around for long either, so make this a lightning lesson." He ejected the second cartridge and handed the gun to Willie. "Now, hold it like this." He guided Willie's hands into the correct position, then stood behind him. "Now close the gun and raise it to your shoulder." They made the movement together several times. "Good, now aiming. Tuck your cheek in against the stock. That's it. Keep both eyes open and look down the barrels and beyond at your target. OK."

"I think so."

"All right. I'll load you. Now remember to release the safety catch, there, before you squeeze the triggers. That's number one, that's two. And pull the butt hard into your shoulder or you'll get a kick you won't like." He slipped in two cartridges. "Now, in your own time, blow that clump of rushes to blazes. But think carefully what you're doing, Willie. Right, go."

He closed the gun, raised it to his shoulder and squeezed the trigger. Nothing happened.

"What the hell?"

"Good thing you're not being attacked by an elephant, Willie boy! The safety catch!"

"Oh aye."

He tried again, detonated a cartridge successfully, but forgot to grasp the butt tightly enough.

"Christ! That hurt."

"It would. Final drill: pull in the butt, Willie."

This time all went well. The Major slid in two more cartridges and they walked on briskly. Soon enough Gypsy flushed another rabbit. Willie methodically closed the gun, raised it, released the safety catch and fired. He missed but, keeping his eyes on the fleeing animal fired again and brought it down.

"That's what I call a cool head. Well done, Willie!"

"It's a bloody good feeling, isn't it," said a grinning Willie, ejecting the spent cartridges as if he'd been doing it for years.

The shot rabbit was again a myxomatosis victim, as was one other the Major killed just before they came back to the fire at Dungearie House.

The Major stood with his back to the marble mantelpiece, rubbing his hands.

"I think we deserve a drop of the guid stuff after our arctic safari, eh, Willie?"

"Wouldn't say no, Major."

"Twelve year old Macallan suit?"

"Beautiful."

Two generous measures were poured into heavy Stuart crystal glasses. They drank. Willie discovered he was out of tobacco. He'd intended to buy some when the Major had picked him up.

"Never fear! Will a Bolivar do? Don't keep cigarettes."

"OK. Thanks very much."

A cigar was removed from the sideboard humidor and handed with a silver cutter to Willie. He enjoyed an occasional cigar or cheroot and lit up with pleasure. However, after the first inhaled puff he was seized by an embarrassing paroxysm of coughing which went on for some time.

"Dear me," said the Major, "you'd better not smoke those too often."

"Sorry," said Willie, "it's just a wee catch in the chest."

Soon he was savouring the cigar's rich perfection.

"So you liked using the shotgun, Willie?"

"I really did, Major. I have to thank you for the experience."

Major Colquhoun smiled broadly "An experience to be repeated one day, I hope. It's a lovely gun. It was my father's. Perfect balance. One of a matched pair. Purdey sidelocks, you know. He had them with him in India."

"Is that right?" said Willie.

They drank another whisky each. The log fire blazed its heat at them. They drank some more Macallan single malt.

Willie finally said, "I'll have to go, Major. But how can I ... ?"

"Never fear, laddie. I wouldn't take the risk, but Mrs Campbell will drive you down to Milngavie in her car. She lives there. Then you can make your own way home. All right? You don't drive, Willie?"

"I never learned."

They parted with a warm handshake.

In the car Willie made the mistake of answering Margaret Campbell's polite question about his job more fully than was necessary.

"So I do my bit to waken up the readers. Mainly about independence for Scotland... the way we should all be thinking."

Mistress Campbell stiffened perceptibly at the wheel.

"The SNP line? Ach, that's just haivers!"

Willie smiled and was about to respond, but the woman snorted derisively and continued, "I wouldnae gie tuppence for thon Nationalists. A gang o' Johnnie Raws wi' as much idea how to behave as... as yon lollypop lady over there."

Willie laughed. "But Margaret, they're your own folks. Anyhow, they're not all..."

She dismissed any defence. "See, with due respect, Mr Devine, they're not *gentlemen*. No' many any road. And as for some o' their females! Screamin' bizzums. They're just chancers, the lot o' them." She snorted again. "No, no. We need a proper government tae rule us Scotch."

Willie managed another smile. "You mean a government of English MPs in London, don't you, Margaret?"

She glanced uneasily at him. "Well, no exactly. I mean, if there was more like the Major... well, mebbe... Here! This is where I'll drop you. There's a bus stop."

Just before he got out, Willie patted her gloved hand companionably. "Thanks for the lift." He gave her another kindly smile. "You are an old snob, Margaret. We're going to have to reconstruct you." He closed the door before she could reply.

Gill was waiting for him when he reached Rubyvale Street about eight. Sleety snow was falling.

"Where've you been, Willie? You look positively windswept!"

"Dungearie House."

"Well I'm damned! The last place I imagined."

He described his afternoon with relish. Gill was delighted that he'd got on so well with her grandfather.

"He's a perfect dear, isn't he, Willie?"

"Aye. You're lucky in him all right, Gill. Now what have *you* been up to? You've got that secret look about you ... I can tell."

"Willie, I've been up to Dr McCabe."

"And?"

"I'm pregnant."

## EIGHT

WILLIE AND GILL REMEMBERED an occasion two months earlier when Willie's sex precautions had proved unreliable during the wild, self-forgetting transports of their love making. Gill had not been taking the contraceptive pill but it was remarkable, nevertheless, to find that one slip had produced this result.

"When did you suspect, Gill?"

"A month ago. But I waited a further full five weeks before I went for a check."

"God! I'm sorry, darling. Were you worried? You should have told me before."

"No, somehow it didn't really bother me. Actually, at times I've felt absurdly happy."

He kissed her tenderly.

For a whole day any question of future arrangements was side-stepped by them both. Finally Willie said, "Would you move in here? That way I can keep an eye on you."

"D'you want that, Willie?"

"Sure. Will you?"

"All right. I'll tell Cathie."

"Fine. And ... will you be telling anyone else?" He jerked a thumb in the vague direction of Bearsden.

"That I'm moving to this address, yes. The other matter, no. Not yet anyway. Please you keep it quiet too, Willie. I've got to get used to the idea!" She smiled at him.

"Mum's the word. Sorry! I'll rephrase that: my lips are sealed."

They laughed.

Gill wrote to Muirlaw Drive. Muriel was outraged and replied saying so. She was aware, she informed Gill, that some young people nowadays flitted about promiscuously, living here and there shamelessly. But she had not thought ever to see a daughter of hers behaving in this way. The one saving grace appeared to be that no mention was being made of marriage. She sincerely hoped Gill would soon come to her senses and get her life back on to a sane footing once more.

Gill handed the letter to Willie.

"About what you'd expect, Gill?"

"Yes."

"How do you react though?"

"I don't. It's pointless getting upstage with her. I don't want to waste my energy."

Willie handed back the letter. "No, I understand. That's not what I meant."

"Sorry?"

"The marriage bit, Gill."

"Oh, that."

They looked at one another steadily for a few moments.

"To be quite straight, I haven't been thinking along those lines. What about you, Gill?"

"Likewise. I haven't really considered it either."

"Frankly, I've got extremely mixed feelings about the institution. I'm not saying I mightn't get round to the notion one day but, right now, there's so much going on that ... well, it just doesn't seem to be on my menu. But listen, Gill, I don't want to do anything which will make you unhappy. I mean if ..."

"Relax, Willie. I'm content just to live with you as long as you love me and will promise to help with the baby when it comes."

Impulsively he crossed the room to hug her. She saw that there were sudden tears in his dark blue eyes.


The little group in the Argyle disintegrated. Since the night of the

Halliday celebration Tommy Bell had not been seen. Rumour had it that he and Nettie had decided to leave the district for the more salubrious avenues of Victoria Park. Lex and Mo seemed to be busy elsewhere most evenings.

Gill had stopped drinking, but on the odd occasion that she and Willie went into the pub the only old face there was usually Hamish MacCorquodale's. Deserted by his erstwhile companions, he was nowadays stationed at the bar conducting a disjointed conversation with the busy barman, Wally Torrance. However, as soon as they appeared Hamish detached himself to join them at a table.

"Ah, Willie! And Chillian MacIntyre: you're looking bonnier each time I see you, and that's the truth, girl."

"Hello, Hamish, you old flatterer."

"Not so much of the 'old', Chillian, if you please." His bespectacled brown eyes twinkled. The mop of red hair was becoming alarmingly unruly, thought Gill, amused.

"What happened to Lex?" asked Willie

"Well, you may search me, I'm sure. All private, his and Mo's activities, seemingly. They won't say, but I've an idea."

"What's that, Hamish?" said Gill.

"Political. Cloak and dagger stuff."

"I see."

Willie said nothing.

MacCorquodale continued, "I don't understand why such an interest means you have to drop your friends, do you, Willie?"

"No. But I'm sure they don't mean it that way, Hamish. They're just occupied, I suppose."

"Aye, well maybe," said the obviously disgruntled MacCorquodale. "I hope they know what they're doing." He turned to Gill. "When I was a bit younger, ten or twelve years ago, there was the Siol Nan Gaidheal – Seed of the Gael, you understand – then Arm Nan Gaidheal. Maniacs that went around with hooded drummers and wearing kilts and carrying dirks and all that. They said they wanted to defend Gaelic culture and tried to achieve it by throwing petrol bombs and getting arrested. Bloody lot of good that did!"

"Set *back* their cause, I'd say."

"Chust exactly that, Chillian. Damned idiots! They alienated thousands of sympathisers."

Gill glanced anxiously at Willie as she asked MacCorquodale, "You don't think Lex or Mo could be involved in anything like that, do you, Hamish?"

He sighed and pushed back his glasses. "As I told you, I seem to have been dropped."

When they left the pub, the shaggy Hamish MacCorquodale looked lonely as he made his way back to Walter at the bar.

At Rubyvale Street Mrs Skelly, in her night-time curlers, met them on the tenement stair. "It's yoursels then? Here's a wee bowl o' soup for ye, Gill. It's gude broth. Ah made it masel." Had she guessed? "Mr Devine, that bloody phone o' yours his been gaun a' night. Couldnae help hearin' it. Through yer flair, like."

"Thanks very much, Mrs Skelly. We'll have to get an ansaphone, won't we?" said Gill.

"Whit? Oh aye, right enough. Well, cheerio." She shuffled away in her tangerine acrylic carpet slippers.

Gill put the kettle on. "Who d'you think it was?"

"Haven't a clue. Anyway, we're back now if they're that desperate."

But there were no further calls that night.


Gill's next telephone conversation was at Rowley Street.

"Jamie here, Gill. Sorry to ring you at school but there's never anybody in when I try your flat."

Should she tell him straight out about her move to Rubyvale Street? Gill hesitated. It was none of his business really. And yet, he was going to find out soon. But no, she'd say nothing for the minute. "Oh hello, Jamie," she responded evenly.

"Are you fit and well, Gill?"

"Plodding on, you know."

He laughed. "That doesn't fit my mental picture of you at all! Pretty lady," he added, for some reason assuming a mock mid-Atlantic accent. "Listen, I'm finally straight at my place, so I'm having a small dinner party to house-warm it."

"Mmm." How was she going to refuse? Did she have to? Did she want to? Jamie's guests would probably be interesting. She hadn't been to a smart party for ages.

"I'd like you to come, Gill. A week tomorrow. Friday. Are you free?"

She thought of Willie and, unaccountably, of Mrs Skelly. "I'm not dead sure there isn't something else on, Jamie. Can I check?"

"Is it old Willie again?"

"If I could ring you back tomorrow, Jamie?"

"OK then. But do try, Gill."

"I'll let you know. About this time tomorrow."

She conferred with Willie.

"Go if you want to, Gill."

"But I won't if you don't want me to."

"Why should I not? You're a free agent."

"I don't know, Willie. I almost wish you'd ask me not to go."

"I wouldn't do that, sweetheart. Jamie what's-his-name's an old friend of yours. There'll be others there. Anyhow, I trust you, Gill, as I hope you trust me. Go if you feel you'll enjoy it."

"I wish you were coming with me."

"Don't be daft! If I did, James might not get to hold your hand. No, no, it's more your scene, Gill."

She accepted the invitation.

Jamie greeted her warmly. "Come in! Let me take your coat, Gill. The others are here. Right, you know the way. I'll introduce you."

Before entering the main room she knew that Charlotte Cholmondley-Pickersgill was there. Her theatrical tones were unmistakeable. "Oh you've *been* to St Lucia, Alec! Isn't it simply *heaven*?"

"Charlotte, Alec," said Jamie. "You remember Gillian MacIntyre? Our launch party?"

Ptarmigan whisky, Gill recalled.

Alec Beattie's polite confirmation was eclipsed by Charlotte's, "Of course, Gill! How *splendid* to see you again. I'm not sure if you've met my friendy-wendy Guy here, have you?" Gill shook her head, smiling. "Ah, then let me present Mr Guy Beaumont!"

They shook hands. Finally Maija, Beattie's willowy, white-blonde Finnish wife, was introduced. "It is very nice to know Jamie's girlfriend, yes?"

"How d'you do, Maija?" Gill replied. "Actually, Jamie and I ..."

"Now, folks, a preprandial snort," said their host quickly. "What's it to be?"

He took orders and withdrew to the small kitchen.

This was all very pleasant. Gill felt comfortable in a smart new, dark green dress. Quite a snappy wee number. The others had all made an effort too. Jamie himself was slimly handsome in navy suit, boldly striped shirt and floral Italian silk tie. Alec Beattie, in a burgundy velvet smoking jacket, artistically complemented his Maija's pink fine corduroy jumpsuit. Charlotte, predictably dramatic, had squeezed herself into a sort of Tudor, vaguely tapestried garment, notable mainly for an abbreviation of material in the area of her well-developed breasts. Guy Beaumont's neatly-cut pinstripe suit was unobtrusive and Gill recognized his old Etonian tie. A pair of lightweight circular tortoise shell-framed spectacles perched on Guy's nose: he looked intelligent, studious.

Beattie said, "Jamie tells me you live in Jordanhill, Gill. Whereabouts? I know it well."

Oh God! So soon. "Yes, temporarily, Alec," she found herself lying. "Munro Road, with a teacher colleague."

"Isn't that rather up-market?" asked Charlotte, rolling her eyes in an irritating gesture Gill remembered from their last encounter.

"Not really," said Gill. Jamie appeared in the doorway with a tray of drinks. Gratefully she jumped up. "Let me help you, Jamie."

"Thanks, Gill. Sorry you're on the tomato juice. Nothing wrong, is there?"

"No, nothing. I don't know why, but I just seem to have gone off alcohol recently," she lied for the second time in a few minutes. Was this going to be the pattern all evening? Gill felt suddenly shaky. Could she keep it up?

Jamie sought her help in the kitchen with the dinner's final preparations. They could not avoid touching one another as they moved about in the confined space. Once he grasped her waist and kissed the back of her neck enthusiastically. Gill shuddered.

The main course was a bubbling cheese fondue, greeted with cries of delight.

"First hit it on a Fettes ski trip in Wengen when I was fifteen. Been hooked ever since. You must use genuine Gruyère and put in a good slug of Kirsch." Jamie gave the dish a proprietorial stir.

"Yummy yum yum!" squeaked Charlotte, skewering a cube of French bread and tentatively twisting it in the molten cheese.

The savoury aroma was delicious. After Jamie had raised his glass of chilled moselle and wished his guests "Buon Appetito!," they fell to eating with relish. Conversation was minimal for some time.

"Wow, Jamie!" said Beattie licking his lips, "how'd you like a job in our boardroom kitchen? This whacks the cook's usual output. And she's a *very* fancy cordon bleu Miss."

Laughter all round.

"D'you drink Ptarmigan whisky with *every* course in your company's dining room, Alec?"

"I don't think any of us ever touch the stuff till after sundown, Charlotte."

"How frightfully imperial of you!"

More laughter. The party was going well.

After frozen raspberries, meringues and cream, Gill readied a cafetière of Douwe Egberts coffee. Jamie placed a decanter of port on the table and glasses at each place, except Gill's. Guy and Maija also declined, on grounds of breathalyser hazard. No-one smoked.

"You are also Scotch, Guy?" asked Maija.

"Half. My mother's side."

"So always you live in England, yes?"

"Again, half and half really. At school and university south of the Border. And my father's home was in Hampshire. Near Liss actually. But I spent a lot of time up at our place in Inverness-shire. West of Beauly it was."

"'Was', Guy?"

"Yes, I'm sorry to say, Alec. I loved the place. Loads of space. The fishing. I got on with the people. Oh, we had marvellous times."

"You sold up?"

"No option. The old man got slaughtered at Lloyds."

Jamie passed the port on to Charlotte. "Your father was a Name?"

"Right. And Mother. Carted for over a million between them. The lawyers are still trying to salvage something, suing all and sundry – without much hope though. Anyhow, the estate had to go."

"A tragedy!" Charlotte injected into the slightly awkward silence which ensued. "Before that your people really were jolly oofy, weren't they, Guy dear?"

"How you say, Charlotte – 'oofy'?" Maija frowned with a combination of commiseration and puzzlement.

"Jolly fucking rich." Charlotte bent forward, providing the company with a disturbingly extensive glimpse of moulded breasts, the pale skin by now faintly roseate owing to the port and the room's warmth. "That's what I mean." Once more she rolled her eyes pointlessly.

"Yes, of course. Thank you, Charlotte," said the embarrassed Maija.

"What did you do at university, Guy?" enquired Gill.

"A PPE degree. Just got through before the sky fell in. Oxford. Magdalene."

"And then?"

"I found my way into estate agenting with Day Francis – you know?"

"Yes. In London?"

"For a bit, but they decided to open in Edinburgh, so I jumped at it. They reckoned I should know something about Scottish country properties."

"But you're in Glasgow now?" said Beattie.

"There just wasn't sufficient turnover in the sector to justify me there. A lot of time on my hands. I managed to read nearly all Dostoevsky, Aldous Huxley and Allan Massie! Then they sent me here to St Vincent Street. Exclusively commercial business. Office blocks, warehousing etcetera. Dull, but lucrative."

"So you're not really a 'white settler', Guy?" said Gill.

Jamie raised and dropped his hand in slight annoyance.

"No," replied Guy, "I don't consider myself such. I will say though, Gill, that I entirely understand that type of resentment."

"Jamie thinks the Scots who complain about English people coming to live here and doing well are just whingers."

"That's right," said Jamie with an emphatic nod. "They should get off their backsides and quit bellyaching if they want to compete."

"If I may say so, I believe that's a slightly tired cliché." Guy Beaumont adjusted his spectacles. "In my opinion it's a complex matter. There should be more assistance for new local enterprises. Maybe some limitation on imported expertise. Better training schemes in Scotland."

Charlotte's mouth was open. "Good God, Guy! I didn't know you felt like that. Positively passionate."

"Well, I'm afraid, Guy, that I regard that sort of talk as negative, not to say crap! With due respect." Jamie waved his hands about.

Beattie said, "We don't seem to need many outsiders in the whisky business. Just a few terribly nice young men down in the St James's premises – principally to deal with American tourists. But I suppose whisky's maybe a special case."

"Quite, Alec," said Jamie, encouraging Charlotte to move the decanter on to him. "If people just take charge of their affairs and stop moaning, they can get ahead all right." He really didn't want this line of discussion to continue.

However, Guy was now looking animated. "You see, that's just the trouble. The Scots are *not* in charge of their affairs."

Charlotte swallowed some port. "It appears I've been consorting with a raging Nationalist! You should have worn a kilt tonight, Guy. I'd love to see your gorgeous little knobbly white knees in the MacBeaumont tartan. Hoots!"

All sitting round the table laughed with relief. However, it appeared that Guy's sense of the ridiculous was less developed than that of the others: after a polite grin in Charlotte's direction, he continued calmly, "Since I've been living properly in Scotland I've detected a thoroughly frustrated feeling about the place. People seem to me apathetic or downright angry. I mean about government from Westminster. They want change."

"Here we go again," said Jamie heavily, becoming irritated with the persistent Guy. "Are you another who's itching to create an Edinburgh Assembly and install a Labour dictatorship?"

"Steady on, Jamie," Beattie interjected. "You'd undoubtedly get a big Labour majority if it was merely a *Devolved Assembly*, but if we were talking about an independent Scottish *Parliament* there could be a much more diverse composition."

"Why should you think that, Alec?"

"Well, I'm no politician but it seems to me that this increasing support for Labour in Scotland in recent years has mirrored an increasing desire for self-government, which the Westminster Tories won't concede. Protest voting. If there were to be a Scottish Parliament I don't see why in due course its elected members wouldn't represent differing strands of opinion in the country, especially if Proportional Representation comes in. The Constitutional Convention's going to make sure that new franchise arrangements produce truly representative membership in the new Parliament."

"Don't tell me you're a Nationalist too, Alec?" asked Charlotte, her bosoms provocatively, but inappropriately, displayed, her eyes stretched wide.

Beattie winked at her, as if humouring a child. "No, I'm really all for maximum economic co-operation and mutual defence arrangements with England, etcetera. But I also happen to think that constitutional change is overdue here. If the SNP can force a breakthrough then I reckon they'll do the country a valuable service. Labour's half-cocked ideas for Devolution won't bring about that change. Indeed, they're liable to create extremely unhelpful confusion."

"I absolutely agree, Alec," said Guy. "If Devolution is foisted on Scotland, far more questions will be asked than answered."

"Such as?" said Gill. This Guy was brighter than she'd thought. Quite handsome too.

"Well, there's the fundamental legal position for starters. Presumably a Scottish Assembly would operate under Scots Law. If so, would it be willing to continue with the system whereby the House of Lords is the ultimate court of appeal? In civil cases anyway. The question of boundaries to determine ownership of North Sea oil, and therefore the division of tax revenues from it, are incredibly complex. It's not *certain* Scotland would be better off. Now, if it's Devolution, maybe those type of issues don't arise so obviously but then, how many Scottish MPs would still go to Westminster versus the Edinburgh Assembly? And would the London representatives have a vote on English laws? If they did, would the English members be able to vote on Scottish laws? The jolly old 'West Lothian Question'. Anyway, what about the *English* regions? Why should they sit back and see the Scots have it both ways? I'm sure they wouldn't. There'd be all kinds of unhelpful jealousies. Another thing: Labour are proposing much less power for a later Welsh Assembly than the Scottish one. If I were a Welshman I'd be deeply insulted. No, Devolution would be an utter mess, a bugger's muddle. That's my view anyway."

Charlotte broke the silence which followed this speech. "Christ! Anyone read any good books lately?"

Jamie replied: "Guy, I think you've made out a perfect case for ignoring the SNP *and* Labour. It's all far too complicated and it's bloody high time the Scots woke up and recognized which side their bread's buttered!"

Guy began again, "I didn't mean to imply ... "

"Oh, drop it, man!" Jamie waved his hands again, vigorously, to end the debate. "I'll tell you one book I have *not* read recently, Charlotte, and that's the wonderful Halliday Award winner."

"Oh, is that that lavatorial thing full of naughty words? *Climbing the Wall* or something? I saw a review. It sounded *disgusting.*"

"*Those Shining Walls* by Tommy Bell, Charlotte," Beattie informed her. "I started it but gave up before half way. Not my bag at all, but I felt I should know about it, being the work of a Glasgow author."

Gill was perspiring. Should she say something? Jamie was watching her. He'd met Tommy in the Argyle that time. His withering dismissal of the book had been deliberate, aimed subtly at her. If she spoke up and told them of her acquaintance with the author it might well lead to further enquiries about her present life. She made no comment. For the third time that evening she experienced an uncomfortable sense of shame, that she was here in these people's company enjoying herself on false pretences. A sudden weariness touched her.

Maija Beattie had been sitting very quietly through most of the conversation. She now said, quite loudly: "I don't know Scottish books but I like to say something else. You all talk about Scottish Parliament and make many problems, many arguings. In Finland we have independent parliament long time now and make happy country, good standards of living. I think Scotland has same population like Finland, maybe five millions of peoples, yes? And Scotland have good resources and clever citizens so where is problem to separate from England, which is a different kind of country?"

Guy clapped. "Brilliant, Maija! Brilliantly put."

Jamie rubbed his brow with vexation. "OK. Look, I think we've had quite enough politics for tonight. Alec, a last glass? Charlotte? Gill, help yourself to another chocolate truffle."

The party soon broke up.

"Thanks, Jamie, I enjoyed myself. And I think you've got the flat very nice," said Gill.

"Right, I'll run you home."

"No, don't bother, Jamie. I'll be fine."

"I insist, Gill. It's late."

"But ... you know, you've had a drink."

"Och, I'm all right. Anyhow, Jordanhill's no distance." He had his car keys in his hand. The front door was open. "Come on."

She was going to have to tell him. To go through the charade of being dropped off at Cathie's address, not to ask him in, then to look furtively for a taxi once he'd driven off – no, it was unthinkable. Was she ashamed of Willie, of living in Partick? No she was not. Willie was at least the equal of any of them.

They got into the Mercedes.

"You must have been pleased with tonight, Jamie? That fondue was superb."

"Too much politics, as usual. What's got into folks nowadays? If we'd been in Fulham or Islington the talk would actually have been interesting. You know, real life matters like careers, holidays, music, who's going out with whom. Not bloody boring Devolution etcetera." He spoke without his usual jaunty humour.

"Oh well," said Gill sympathetically. Now for it. "Incidentally, Jamie, I'm not actually in Jordanhill any more."

"No?"

"I've moved to Partick. Rubyvale Street if you know it?"

For a moment nothing was said.

"I don't suppose this move had anything to do with Mr Willie Devine?"

"You might as well know, Jamie, I'm living with him. Last month we decided ..."

He brought the Mercedes to an abrupt halt and turned to look at her. His eyes stared. "Do you mean to tell me you're actually living with that common prick of a reporter?"

"Jamie, I think we should ..."

"And you had the cheek to accept my invitation, to sit at my table and accept hospitality, to be introduced to my friends? I can't believe it. By Christ! I feel like ..."

"Jamie, please! Don't be so angry." Gill was beginning to cry. "I know I should have told you before but ..."

"Get out!"

"But Jamie ..."

"Get out of the fucking car right now, you bloody bitch, or I'll ... I'll... *Get out*!" He screamed.

Gill did what she was told and watched the Mercedes disappear at high speed. She stepped into a gloomy close mouth and stifled her weeping with her handkerchief. Oh God! How stupid she'd been. How *could* she have expected to participate in an evening like that, as Jamie Ballantyne's partner too, given her present commitment to Willie? But did that mean she had to exclude herself from all such affairs in the future? It probably did. Certainly she mustn't send out the wrong signals to any other man.

More or less calm again, she began walking to Rubyvale Street. There were few people about at this hour, almost one a.m., just enough to prevent her from feeling apprehensive. She'd be glad to get back to Willie. Gill thought about him, unconsciously comparing him with those in whose company she'd been so recently. She decided that this was profitless: there were too many obvious differences. The only area of overlap was politics, the contemporary politics of Scotland. She herself now definitely shared Willie's conviction that constitutional change should be happening. Guy Beaumont, Alec Beattie, and Maija too probably agreed. Jamie clearly did not. Charlotte didn't count.

So why did the quality of Willie's opinions seem to her so much weightier? Yes, he was a prominent journalist and more directly involved than the others – was that it? She walked on. As she neared home Willie's presence became almost tangible to her. She could hear his voice in her head. Then it came to her: Willie was *doing* things, actively trying to *precipitate* events, while those others merely talked – they *awaited* events.

He was in bed.

"Is that you, Gill? You OK?"

"Yes, Willie. Don't let me disturb you."

She undressed quickly in the dark and slipped in beside him.

"I came to bed early," he said. "Wasn't feeling too good."

"Oh? What's wrong?"

"Don't know. Sort of pains all over. Probably 'flu."

"I'm sorry, Willie. Can I get you anything?"

"It's all right. I took a bloody great glass of whisky. That's the best medicine. Just you please spoon into my back. That's what I want, sweetheart." He gave a little chuckle. "Both of you."

She put her arms around him. "Should you take tomorrow off, darling man?"

"Maybe. I'll see. Let's sleep."

Soon they were both unconscious, warm and breathing deeply.

The ringing of the phone just after two a.m. knifed through the silence.

"Who the blazes ... ? I'm ..." grumbled Gill.

But Willie was out of bed already. "Leave it to me!" he commanded. Seconds later he was back in the bedroom, urgently pulling on his clothes. "I've got to get to the office *immediately*," he said.

"What is it, Willie?"

"Och, never mind." He looked at her steadily for a moment. "Well, I suppose you'll hear soon enough. There's been a big explosion in George Square!"

## NINE

HALF AN HOUR EARLIER a neutrally grey-painted van had been
quietly parked in the shadows, behind the City Chambers abutting
on George Square. Minutes later, when it was clear that the area was
deserted, two figures left the van and hurried silently through a smirr
of cold rain towards the broad-fronted General Post Office on the
south side of the square. They wore gloves. One carried a heavy
suitcase. At a corner they separated. The unencumbered man quickly
crossed the road to the front entrance, took a key from his pocket
and unlocked a small door. He looked around stealthily, then
signalled to his companion to join him. In seconds they were both
inside the building, the door left just ajar.

They knew exactly where they were going. Over many weeks of
rehearsal laborious study of an amateur floor plan, drawn up by a
GPO employee accomplice, had ensured that they moved with
minimum delay. They located the main concentration of
administrative offices, gingerly opened the case, pushed it in the
dark up against a row of filing cabinets and activated a switch
mechanism. In the silence of the great building the men's harsh
breathing sounded frighteningly loud. They had to get out, now, fast.

One individual retraced his steps to the front door, took an
envelope from his pocket and dropped it on the floor of the
cavernous entrance hall. Then he stepped outside and ran for the
waiting van.

The other man hurried down a long corridor, silent in trainers,
took another key out and secured his own escape via a door in the
rear of the building. He too ran with all his strength, down Glassford

Street, along Trongate and south down the Saltmarket. Near the Clyde he located a telephone kiosk, and then paused, panting.

The noise and force of the explosion astonished him. "Holy Christ!" he muttered, getting out coins for the phone. He stretched a handkerchief over the mouthpiece.

"Hullo. The balloon's gone up! Helluva fuckin' bang! Totally successful, I'd reckon. Message delivered an' a'. OK. Over tae you, boy."

Willie put the finishing touches to his article in the back of the cab. He went straight to Gilbert Rankin, the Night Editor.

"Gibby! Hold everything! I've got a new front page for you. First edition, mind! We'll have to shift ourselves."

"What're you on about, Willie?"

He explained the bare story. "I've drafted out roughly what I think we should say."

"Drafted? This looks to me as if you've been working on it for ever, Willie."

"Let's not waste time, Gibby. Just speed-read the piece and see if it needs any changes. I believe we've got a good old-fashioned scoop here, Gibby!"

Rankin had had high hopes when he joined the *Glasgow Recorder*, but it had rapidly become clear that he was condemned to play second fiddle to Sandy Black, the well-ensconced incumbent, and to work the Night Editor's unsocial hours. Sometimes Gibby felt wild with envy and frustration. As he read Willie's piece his heart began to thump.

"You sure about this explosion?"

"Absolutely."

"There's nothing through yet. On the screens."

"That's the point, Gibby! This is gold-plated information."

"How d'you know it's political? What is it, Willie? Some kind of crazy Nationalist splinter group."

"I don't have any labels, Gibby. All I know is what I've written."

"Oh aye, I'll believe that, Willie. What d'you think I am?"

"Gibby, I don't care if you're fuckin' Donald Duck! *Are you going to run it or not?*" He waited a moment. "I don't think Black would want us to miss a story like this."

Rankin picked up the phone to the Production Manager. "Don't worry, Willie, I'll run it all right. Go on, get on with it!"

When Willie had left Rankin informed the night girl on the switchboard that he'd be out for half an hour or so. Then he drove to George Square. Or, more exactly, its environs since the square and adjacent streets were cordoned off and police were everywhere. He showed his press card to a young constable.

"Sorry, sir. I can't let you through."

"I'll go on foot. I need to check some facts."

"No, I'm sorry, sir, but our instructions are not to let anyone through on any pretext whatsoever."

"OK. What do you know about this? Was it a bomb? Could it have been a gas explosion?"

"I don't know anything, sir." Rankin began to walk away. He wasn't going to get any change. The constable relented a little and called after him, "I'm quite sure there's nothing wrong with the gas system, sir."

Right, that was enough. There *had* been a big explosion, probably at the GPO, and it *was* almost certainly a bomb. Devine's story rang true. He must be on the inside track. He'd not make mistakes over a massively important event like this. Not Devine. Gilbert Rankin harboured a healthy, if unspoken respect for Willie's professionalism.

By six a.m. the first issues of the *Recorder* were on the streets of Glasgow. The front page screamed its message:

*BOMBERS!*

A huge bomb was detonated at George Square's General Post Office in the early hours of this morning. The perpetrators of this outrage are as yet unknown, but a suspicion is growing that the motive may have been political.

The *Recorder* has been warning for some
time now that, if frustration with Westminster
among the Scottish people was allowed to reach
a dangerous intensity, something like this was
bound to happen. It is a mercy that the bombers
seem to have deliberately selected a time and
place where it was relatively safe to make their
demonstration. Remembering the Easter Rising
of 1916, the GPO looks a significant choice.

When will the Tories in far-off London wake
up to Scotland's demand for self-government?
When will Labour realize that the shabby,
toothless compromise of Devolution is not ac-
ceptable here?

Are we to face twenty five years of terrorism
and violent bloodshed, on the Northern Irish
pattern, before the politicians get the message?
Surely not? The Scottish people are decent, law-
abiding folk at heart, but God help their enemies
if they once get their dander up!

While the *Recorder* can never condone illegal
actions, perhaps the explosion of anger in
George Square this morning will at last force the
main political parties into realistic and early dis-
cussions about the future government of Scot-
land.

On his way home at breakfast time Willie noticed with wry pleasure
the placarded headlines of competitor newspapers: 'New Bosnian
Ceasefire', 'Edinburgh Olympic Bid', 'Fresh Sex Scandal Rocks
Palace'. He knew Sandy Black was going to blow his top but it was
worth it for this. He'd scooped the lot! His newspaperman's ego was
fully inflated and he was relishing it. But there was a much deeper
satisfaction too. However the others might choose to present, to
interpret, the bombing, he'd got in first, he'd set the tone firmly

along the desired lines. By God, he was going to enjoy his breakfast with Gill! Bacon, eggs, mushrooms. He'd pick up some Lorne sausage at the butcher. Willie's adrenalin was still pumping.

The TV was on and Gill was sitting in front of it. She rose and embraced Willie emotionally.

"Oh, my darling! I've been so worried. It's terrible!"

"Calm down, pet. What are they saying?"

"Awful damage to the Post Office computer centre."

"So?"

"One man killed. They've caught two of the bombers."

Willie sagged into a chair. "Oh no, no, no, *no!*" He brought his clenched fist down on the chair arm with all his strength.

"Here's another news flash. Listen."

> *"We take you over to our correspondent, Joan Hastie, in George Square. Joan, is the position any clearer now?"*
>
> *"Yes, Michael, it's beginning to fall into place. Just to recap, it appears the terrorists belong to a small group calling themselves the 'Free Scotland Brigade', the FSB. The police found a message from them. I'll read it out. It's quite short. 'We, The Free Scotland Brigade, demand on behalf of the Scottish people the right to govern ourselves. The Union Treaty of 1707 is now a cruel prison in which the Scottish nation is shackled while England sucks our blood. The Treaty was not agreed to by all the Scottish people in the first place. The Labour Party's offer of Devolution within the Union is a sham which will lead to endless wasteful arguments. The Tories' insistence on maintaining the Act of Union is totally unacceptable, and they have absolutely no mandate from the Scottish people. Scotland*

*demands an Independent Parliament - NOW! If this is not soon seen to be a genuine possibility, the FSB gives due warning that further bombings will take place'."*

*"Thanks, Joan. Is there any reaction yet from The Scottish National Party?"*

*"Their spokesman has completely disassociated the SNP from the FSB. He said that the party had never heard of them."*

*"And the Conservatives and Labour?"*

*"No comments as yet, Michael."*

*"Right. Now the victim. What do we know about him? Any more details?"*

*"As I said before, he was a security guard called Charles McKillop, aged twenty five. He was on his rounds in the GPO and seems to have discovered the bomb just when it went off at 2 a.m. We've now learned that he was married with two small children, girls, both under five."*

*"It's a terrible tragedy, Joan."*

*"The crowds round here are very upset, Michael. I've seen quite a few people openly crying."*

*"Yes ... Tell me, Joan, is there anything yet on the captured men?"*

*"Not officially, Michael. The police are saying nothing. There's a rumour going round that one of them may be an Asian, but I've no confirmation of that I must emphasize."*

*"Fine, thank you, Joan Hastie. We'll be back to you if there are any new developments."*

Willie slumped further in his chair. His unshaven face was deadly pale. There were deep lines about his mouth. "Switch the thing off

NOW YOU MUST DANCE

for God's sake, Gill," he said weakly.

All he could manage to eat was some toast and black coffee, followed by several cigarettes and much coughing. At eight, Black was on the phone.

"I have to go back to the office, Gill. Sandy Black's going ape."

"Oh, Willie, take care, won't you?" Gill was shaking in alarm.

He smiled heartbreakingly and kissed her with great tenderness. "Don't fret, darling. I'll be all right."

"Willie," she whispered, "I adore you."

When he'd gone Gill lay down on their bed and wept.

Black was in an incandescent rage.

"You bloody liar, Devine!"

"Sandy, what d'you ..."

"You gave your word to me and Graham Harbottle you'd be even-handed in these political matters."

"You mean the bomb story?"

"Of course I do! Don't play fucking games, Willie. Not with me."

"I reported what I heard."

"No you didn't. You turned it into a political platform. Quite unjustified."

"But, Sandy, it *is* a political story. You'll have heard the TV announcement? The FSB statement?"

"Yes, yes, but that's not the point."

Willie shook his head. "I'm not with you."

"Aw, cut the crap, Willie! You do a whitewash job on a horrendous, a murderous crime and throw a lot of shit over Labour's Devolution policy – and you sit there kidding on you don't understand what's wrong. Who the hell d'you think you are? Rupert fucking Murdoch?"

"No, Sandy, thank Christ."

"Well, I happen to be directly responsible to the Board, Willie Devine. And I'd lay any money they're not going to like this front page one little bit. A front page you slipped by me incidentally. Absolutely without my authorization. Just don't you forget that! If Harbottle tells me ..." The phone on his desk rang. Still glaring at

Willie, he picked it up. "Norman? Yes ... yes, I see ... Uh-huh ... well, you'd better go ahead." He put the phone down. "We'll have to talk about this later. After I've spoken to Graham Harbottle. I'll let you know. Bugger off, Willie."

Willie went to his desk and rang the production manager. "Hi, Norman! How're you doing?"

"Great, Willie. What is it, laddie? Quick, I'm hellish busy the now."

"I just wondered how the sales were today. The bomb story, you know?"

"Fantastic! I've never seen anything like it! We can't keep up. I just got authorization for *another* run. The machines are red hot!"

"Terrific, Norman. It's the bomb story doing it, I suppose?"

"Aye. Did you have anything to do with the front page, Willie?"

"A bit, Norman."

"Fabuloso, boy! Joe Public's obviously got the idea the *Recorder* has the drop on the competition. Keep the material coming, Willie. This could run and run!"

"Great, Norman. I'll do what I can."

Willie sat staring at his terminal screen. A doodling half hour later he called up the list of his recent articles on the constitutional issue, and was soon re-reading key passages. Those pieces had certainly been to the point. Spot on. Restlessly he clicked the mouse.

By lunchtime no further summons to the Editor's office had come, so Willie left.

In the days that followed, the handsomely increased sales level was maintained. The Devine column continued to take the same attitude as the original article, and the *Recorder*'s main editorial line did not seriously contradict it. However, several other press commentators were more clearly condemnatory, and only timidly faced the political significance of the George Square incident. They played it down as the work of the lunatic fringe.

If the Amalgamated Press Group had decided that, on balance, they were not going to complain further about their Mr Devine's conduct during the past week, the Glasgow police were not about to take the same attitude. Willie's presence was required at two thirty in the office of Detective Inspector Kenneth MacAllister.

"Sit down Mr Devine," ordered the choleric-looking MacAllister. "This is Detective Sergeant Wilson." He took a packet of cigarettes out of his tweed jacket pocket. "Smoke?"

"Not just for the minute," said Willie.

"OK." MacAllister spoke slowly to indicate that he had all the time in the world. "Now, Willie – is it all right if I call you Willie, Willie? I've been reading your column for a while now. You're like an old friend, Willie."

Sarcastic bastard. Brutal probably, given half a chance. Willie knew the type. "Fine."

"Right. I'll just stay 'Inspector' to you though, Willie. Right?"

"Right."

"It's important we understand each other from the off, Willie. Isn't that so?"

"Yes, right."

"Have you got that paper, Jim?" The other man handed him a *Recorder*. "Now then, Willie, this is the early edition of your paper on the day of the bombing. Do you recognize the front page?"

"Of course."

"Good. Now Mr Gilbert Rankin – you know him, don't you, Willie?"

"He's the Night Editor."

"Just so. Well, Mr Rankin's told us that you, Willie, were responsible for the front page article. Can you confirm that?"

"Yes. Bar a few small changes, I wrote it."

The Inspector laid down the paper and inhaled and exhaled tobacco smoke in a leisurely manner. "When did you put the story together, Willie?"

"Early on the day in question. As soon as I heard what had happened."

"According to Mr Rankin, you approached him at around three

a.m."

"I don't remember the time."

"Come on, Willie. Mr Rankin's told us. Anyway, Mr Sandy Black says it would have had to be about that time to get the thing set up properly for the first edition. Which this is." He flapped the newspaper up and down.

"I suppose it could have been three."

"Suppose? I hope you're going to find it possible to be more precise than that with other questions I have to ask you. Eh, Willie?" He forced an ugly smile.

"I'll do what I can to help."

"Number one: when were you told a bomb had exploded at George Square at two a.m.?"

"It must have been between two and two thirty."

"Good, Willie. Now, number two, and take your time on this: who told you?"

"That I don't know."

MacAllister hammered the table. "Think again, Willie! And just be aware that Sergeant Wilson here is witnessing this. Don't go telling us any wee fibs. *Understand*?" He shouted.

"I understand."

"OK. Then I'll ask you again. Who was it that told you ... by the way, how did you receive the information?"

"By phone."

"It's as well you said that, Willie, because we've had a tap on your line. You didn't know that, did you, Willie?"

"No."

"So, who was it phoned you that morning between two and two thirty? I want an answer, Willie."

"I can't tell you."

"You must have recognized the voice? Wasn't it one of your friends from the Argyle, Willie? One of your drinking pals?"

"I told you, I didn't recognize the voice." Willie could hear again the indistinct, handkerchief – muffled, 'The balloon's gone up!' as if he had the phone to his ear at that moment. "If you have a recording, can't *you* tell maybe?"

"Don't be cheeky now, Willie, or I might get annoyed." He stubbed out his cigarette with some violence. "I expect you slick newspaper boys think we're a bunch of flat-footed idiots, don't you?"

"No."

"Aw, that's nice of you to say that, Willie. Very communicative, isn't he, Sergeant Wilson?"

"Oh yes," said the subordinate.

"Let's try communicating along a different path, shall we, Willie? What would you say if I told you that you and your pals have been under surveillance for several months?"

"That I was surprised."

"Uh-huh. And what if I told you that we *know* who it was that called you that morning?"

"That you know more than I do."

"Clever bugger, aren't you, Willie."

"Have you caught him, whoever it is?"

"Not yet, but we will. As long as his two accomplices keep co-operating. You're good friends with Mohammed Zafrullah Hossein and Alexander James Grant, aren't you, Willie?"

"I've known them for some years. We drink together."

"So you must have shared all their little secrets, eh?"

"It seems not."

"What the hell did you talk about then?"

"Poetry, literature, women, politics, football."

"And what was the nature of your political discussions?"

"Mainly about Scotland's position in the UK. The need for constitutional change."

"And the activities of the Free Scotland Brigade no doubt?"

"I'd never heard of them till the other day."

"Which day?"

"The day of the bombing. When their message was read out on the TV that morning."

"You really expect us to believe that, Willie?"

"It's the truth."

"So Grant and Hossein acted entirely on their own without telling anyone else?"

"I can't say that, but they didn't tell me."

Willie noticed MacAllister flick his head momentarily at Wilson, who then moved towards the door.

"I think we'll go to another room, Willie, and continue our discussions there. Jim?"

"OK, Ken."

The Inspector stood up and indicated that Willie should do likewise. They prepared to leave when MacAllister hesitated. "Just a minute. There's a question I meant to get into. Sit down again, Willie."

He made to comply. Wilson appeared to help by pushing the chair forward but when Willie sat down the chair had been pulled away. He fell sprawling on the floor. Next moment he felt a hard clubbing kick in his kidneys.

"Oh, I'm sorry, Mr Devine!" said Wilson. "That was clumsy of me."

Pain shot through Willie's body.

"What a shame," said a grinning MacAllister. "There's Sergeant Wilson trying to aid you and we have a wee accident. Too bad." He took out a cigarette and lit it.

Feeling sick, Willie knew he must nevertheless see the interview through somehow. He gritted his teeth. "Mind if I have a fag? A roll-up."

"No, I'd rather you didn't, Willie. We'll have an awful fug in here and Sergeant Wilson's allergic to too much smoke. Isn't that right, Jim?"

"Right, Ken."

"Now, where were we? Oh aye. Listen, Willie, I want you to realize we're basically on your side. D'you understand what I'm saying?"

"Yes." He felt ghastly. Could he hold out? Lex and Mo had obviously talked freely. Pain seemed to press in on him everywhere.

Occasionally his eyes went out of focus for a second.

"See, you've been under surveillance, but so have those other comedians. Lousy lot of fuckin' Papists and Paki bastards!" The man's eyes suddenly blazed. He drew heavily on his cigarette. Eventually he continued, "So we know all your movements, Willie, which means that we know you were not at the scene of the crime and that they were. You may think your information is good, Willie, but I can assure you ours is better."

"Meaning?" With a great effort he affected a composure he did not at all feel.

"We were tipped about the fuckin' caper just ahead of time. It was only a crying shame that that poor security sod had to get killed before we got there. Anyhow, your bomber pals in their wee van ran right into our arms. So you see, Willie, we're very well informed."

"Well done."

"I sincerely hope you're not being sarcastic, Willie?"

"No, not at all."

"All right. Now I'm going to ask you again about that phone call. Think carefully, Willie. I want a straight answer. Who was it that rang you to tell you the balloon had gone up at 2.18 that morning?"

"I've told you, I don't know."

"Christ, Willie! it was Daniel Ramage, wasn't it? Hossein and Grant have told us. Don't go on insulting me by sitting there and denying you know him."

"I don't deny I know him but I'm telling you I do not know who rang with the bombing information. No name was given. It was hard to make out what the person was saying as a matter of fact. But you'll know that if you recorded it."

Suddenly MacAllister looked beaten. "So, you're telling me that Grant and Hossein never told you anything of their plans to bomb the GPO. And some anonymous person rang to tell you when the bomb had exploded, someone whose identity you're quite ignorant of. Is that your story, Devine?"

"It is. And if you ask any journalist, one that deals with sensitive issues anyway, he'll tell you that it's not uncommon for unidentified strangers to make contact with information – if they think you might help in some way."

"Fuckin' bullshit, Devine! Get out of here. For now, that is. We'll be seeing you again if I've got anything to do with it!"

Willie drew on all his reserves. "Inspector MacAllister, and you, Mr Wilson, let me warn *you* now. If you bother me again about this affair you can both expect your names and ugly mugs to be plastered all over the front page of the *Glasgow Recorder*. The subject of the article – Police Brutality. I swear, a description of my first-hand experience will do you no good at all. Do you read me, you *bastards*?"

"Get out, Devine!" MacAllister shouted, "or I'll have you arrested."

"Oh no. You wouldn't dare."

Willie left, mustering what dignity his aching body allowed.

When he reached Rubyvale Street he more of less fell into Gill's arms. Before she was able to guide him to a chair he fainted. Only for half a minute or so, but when he came round his pallor was chalk-like. His bloodshot eyes were black-ringed: Gill knew all too well how little he'd slept during the past nights. She gave him a large measure of whisky and began to cook some mince and potatoes.

"You've got to eat, Willie darling."

"Yes, I know, but I've no appetite."

She asked him about the police interview and he gave her enough detail to indicate how unpleasant it had been, although he decided not to distress her unnecessarily by mentioning the kicking.

"D'you think you satisfied them?"

"I wouldn't put it that way, Gill, but they got no change out of me beyond ... well, I suppose I could stretch a point and say that, actually, I told them all I know."

"So you shouldn't be summonsed again? But what if there's a trial? I mean, Lex and Mo will obviously have to stand trial."

"Maybe they'll ask me for a written statement. I doubt anything beyond that. The police will advise the Prosecution that I'm really no use, that I can't help them."

Gill eyed him with a mixture of anxiety and compassion. She coaxed him into eating a small portion of mince, but he was soon back in his armchair with a cigarette, looking utterly exhausted.

The telephone rang. It was Hamish MacCorquodale. He was in tears.

"Willie! The police has been here chust now. They gave me an awful grilling but I ... Oh God, Willie! Poor Lex and Mo ... I can't believe ..."

"Hamish!" Willie said loudly, "cut the talk. This line's bugged. Meet me in the usual place tomorrow at twelve. OK."

"At twelve? Ah, right you are, Willie." He began making tearful noises again. "Christ, Willie! I'm shaken. I mean, who could have...?"

"Shut it, Hamish! See you tomorrow." He put the phone down. What might MacCorquodale have said? He was an emotional person.

"He's really upset, by the sound of it," said Gill.

"Naturally. He was pretty close to the other two."

"It's ghastly. Almost unbelievable, isn't it."

"It is, Gill." He seemed to crumple before her eyes.

"Listen, Willie Devine. I'm going to *insist* you get into bed this minute. D'you hear?"

But rest had to be further postponed. There was a shuffling outside on the stairhead followed by a gentle knock on the door. Gill answered.

It was little Mr and Mrs Hossein from The Paradise Curry Garden.

"Oh, Miss, is Mr Willie in? Is this his house, please? So sorry to disturb."

Willie was on his feet. "Come in," he said, pulling out two dining-table chairs. "Please sit down."

Mo's father pitched in straight away. "Mr Willie, this is a *terrible* thing has happened!"

"I know. I'm very very sorry, Mr Hossein."

"Mohammed is our only son. Everything we have built is for him. His sisters find husbands. What can we do? What can we do?"

His wife emitted a stifled cry of distress. Gill touched her on the shoulder.

"It's just hellish, Mr Hossein," said Willie hopelessly.

"He was always good boy and we are loving him too much, too much. We've had little arguments maybe. Sometimes he prefers to be a Scotsman to member of Islam. Yes, I think so. But he was always good dutiful son, Mr Willie." Mrs Hossein again squeaked miserably and her husband took her hand in his. "Only trouble, Mohammed is easily led boy. It was always so. This terrible thing happening at the George Square I know for sure he was not doing." He wrung his hands in torment.

"Nobody realized it would turn out such a tragedy, Mr Hossein. I'm sure of that."

"To us Muslims, Mr Willie, life is sacred. Our Mohammed would not be killing persons. He was only driving getaway car. Policeman told us. So he not guilty like others. Is that not so?"

"I don't know enough about the law to answer that, I'm afraid, Mr Hossein."

"You mean Mohammed could be a prisoner for whole life?"

"I can't answer, Mr Hossein."

Although Mo's mother did not speak English fluently, she understood enough to know what was being said. Fluttering her hands she began to wail piteously. Her husband put his arms round her and eventually quietened her sufficiently to speak again.

"Mr Willie, you are Mohammed's friend and a good man. Please to help us. You see how Mrs Hossein is weeping? I am not sure she can bear to live if our son is jailbird. I myself am a man and must hide feelings, but my heart is breaking open with sorrow."

"I wish I *could* help."

"This is what I have to say, sir. We have built good business. I will sell it, maybe £60,000. I can borrow from friends at mosque, also relations in Pakistan. All savings I put in. Grand total up to £100,000, approximately. If we are hungry in our old age – no matter."

"I really don't know what defence lawyers charge."

"Mr Willie, I do not speak of lawyers."

"Well what do you ... ?"

"I am offering *gift* of £100,000 for release of Mohammed. Trouble is I do not know who is right person to offer in police. But clever fellow like you, Mr Willie, you will be knowing. That I am sure."

"Are you talking of a bribe?"

The little man flicked his hands about in the air. "If you like. What are words? This is my son's life!" At last he too gave way to tears. His wife handed him her tissue.

"We can't operate like that in this country, Mr Hossein. I'm sorry. I'll try to ensure they're well defended. But that's all I can promise you ."

"So Mohammed can still go to jail for his lifelong?"

"These days sentences are usually shorter. Maybe twenty years."

Both Hosseins howled in pain.

Next morning in the Argyle there were more tears. Hamish MacCorquodale had to remove his spectacles and wipe his eyes when Willie came in.

"I'm chust in hell, Willie. To think it's no time at all since we were all round this very table having a jolly good laugh. It's bloody awful, isn't it now?"

"The whole business went tragically wrong, Hamish. That's the bottom line. Nobody wanted an innocent man killed. And nobody expected to spend the rest of his life in jail. It was only ever intended as a strong political demonstration. That's as far as I understood it, anyway. Of course I never knew any specific details of what the plans were." He looked searchingly at MacCorquodale. "Did you, Hamish?"

"Och, not really. I guessed a lot, mind you. I heard them whispering something about the GPO once."

"But the timing – had you any idea?"

"No. Except one thing ...." He began to look very sorry for himself again.

"What, Hamish?"

"Well, the night of the explosion Lex and Mo were in here for a bit. I hadn't seen them for quite a while and it was nice to chat again. But after a couple of beers they wouldn't drink any more, barring tonic water or something like that."

"Not like Lex Grant."

"See, it was very noticeable they were keen to stay sober."

"So you put two and two together."

"Maybe sort of subconsciously, you know."

Willie supped his pint thoughtfully. "How much of this did you tell the police, Hamish?"

"Virtually nothing. I couldn't deny knowing those two, but I said that we'd not been so friendly in recent times. Which was true enough."

"Did you say they'd been in here?"

"Well, there were witnesses. No point saying anything else. All I told them was we'd had a drink together, then they'd moved on."

"So that's all they wanted to find out."

MacCorquodale sighed unhappily. "Yes, really. Oh, of course they wanted to be sure of *my* movements too, but that was no problem."

"You just went home to Hillhead from here to sleep, Hamish?"

"Well, not exactly. I was a bit down that night so I stayed till closing time. Then Wally was kind enough to take me back to his place for a wee nightcap or two." MacCorquodale jerked his thumb over his shoulder. "He's a simple chap, Wally, but I've got to like him. I don't have a lot of friends here in Glasgow, you know, Willie. Not that I can relax with anyhow. I get lonely."

"Aye well, Hamish. I see. No, Wally's a good bloke, I agree. Seen it all. Quite the philosopher!"

MacCorquodale smiled, his eyes still tear-stained. "We took a drop too many. I fell asleep till Wally woke me at nearly three o'clock. I walked home. Anyway, at least I had an alibi, no problem, Willie."

They bought one another pints of heavy. Inevitably the conversation moved to the police action in trapping two of the bombers. How had they contrived to be on the spot so promptly. Was it chance? Or had they indeed been tipped off, as MacAllister had claimed? And if so, by whom, in God's name *by whom*? The next morning they had their answer.

Walter Torrance was found on a piece of waste ground near the Clyde: his throat had been cut.

# TEN

*MURDER SEEN AS POLITICAL REVENGE KILLING*

Last night Walter Torrance, 53, a barman at the
Argyle Public House in Dumbarton Road,
Glasgow, was murdered in a savage attack and
his body dumped on vacant ground near the
River Clyde. A message was hung round his
neck which read: 'This is what happens to
Scotland's traitors. Beware! The Free Scotland
Brigade is gaining recruits every day and will
not tolerate betrayal. Our objective of
Independence for Scotland must be achieved at
all costs!' The typewritten message was signed
'High Command HQ, FSB.'

According to a police spokesman, the Argyle
was frequented by the two terrorists recently
apprehended at the George Square GPO bomb
blast which killed a young security guard.

Although the cause of Mr Torrance's death
was by severance of the windpipe, his body
showed widespread contusions and both legs
had been broken. Police are working on the
theory that the assailants tortured Mr Torrance
before executing him, possibly in an effort to
extort information. However, the spokesman did
not say whether the murdered man played any
part in the George Square FSB affair.

Robert MacIntyre shuddered as he read the gruesome report on a VDU in the dealing room. Already Scottish-based quoted companies' prices were being heavily marked down. He'd have to inform a number of his top accounts straight away. Some stop-loss sales might be triggered. Everyone asked the same question: "Is this a one-off maverick business, or is it the beginning of serious civil strife?" Robert had no clear-cut answer to give.

The senior partner of their correspondent firm in the City of London rang in some agitation.

"Mr MacIntyre? Oh Robert, Philip Cherrington here. Are you well, old man?"

"Yes, fine, Philip. And yourself?"

"Jogging along, you know. Look here, Robert, what's all this bloody Freedom Brigade business up there? Or whatever it's called. These bombs, the murder this morning?"

"It's horrible, I know. But I don't ..."

"It's horrible for prices, Robert. That's what we're concerned about down here. I mean, is it serious or is it simply some lunatic fringe having a go?"

"Well, there is a demand for political change in the air, Philip. I'm sure you're aware of that?"

"Yes, yes, I've read something about it, but that's the politicians' bailiwick, Robert. We haven't time to follow every twist and turn of their finagling. What we need to know is whether there's going to be any further trouble. Industrial sabotage maybe?"

Robert set his jaw. "I'm afraid I can't answer that, Philip. For what it's worth, my personal view is that this will blow over. I don't believe it will escalate."

"I hope you're right. Our institutional fund managers have to perform, Robert. They couldn't care less about political grievances and all that stuff. They'll withdraw their backing from companies with significant Scottish operations if the uncertainty isn't removed very quickly. The market's worst enemy, Robert – uncertainty."

"I realize that. It scares off overseas investors too."

"Quite. I hope there'll be an authoritative statement from

someone soon. That's all I can say. Will you be good enough to let me know if there are any developments? One feels a very long way away here from Bonnie Scotland!"

"I'll ring you right away if I learn anything new, Philip."

"Many thanks, old boy. Family all well?"

"Yes thanks. And yours?"

"Blooming thanks. Jessica was just saying it would be nice to see you and Muriel out at Saffron Walden again. 'Bye."

There had been no mistaking the concern in Philip Cherrington's voice. But as the morning moved on no further news item appeared. The *Recorder*'s midday leader made it clear that Walter Torrance had indeed warned the police just before the explosion in George Square, and that his murder had been an FSB reprisal. There was a rather fuzzy picture of Daniel Ramage in several papers and appeals for information from anyone who might have seen him recently.

Robert walked down to the Western Club for lunch. In the bar there was only one topic of conversation.

"The bastards should be strung up when they're caught!" Thus Harry Cuthbertson, a loquacious insurance broker. "Instead of which they'll get a slap on the wrist, plenty of ping-pong and TV, then early release. You watch!"

Affirmatory mumbles.

"I share your outrage, Harry. These terrorists have got to be hunted down and locked away for ever." This was Dr Gordon Renfrew a well-groomed, pin-striped individual with a comfortable berth at the Scottish HQ of a multinational group. "But that won't explain their motives. I mean, they're not simply hooligans from what one can glean."

"That's right, Gordon," said John Yuill, a recently retired gentleman farmer. "These people have real political objectives."

"We *all* have gripes about the politicians, but we don't go around killing people! Surely to God we're not going to start behaving like the IRA?" said Cuthbertson.

"I sincerely hope not, Harry. I spend my time as a doctor *saving* life, but of course if political passions become inflamed ... well ..."

Renfrew lifted his well-cared for hands into the air.

"You mean the dreaded Union/Devolution/Independence nexus?"

"Right, Harry."

Robert spoke: "This kind of thing is deadly for the market. Scottish enterprises. Overseas companies with operations here. Who's going to invest in something that might be blown up next week?"

John Yuill was a thoughtful man. "The authorities must act. Get on top of terrorism if it looks like spreading – I'm not saying it will, mind you, but you never know how things can get out of hand. Then, *soon*, they have to negotiate a new constitutional settlement."

"Devolution?" Cuthbertson queried. "But Labour are already committed to that and they're going to get in at the next election, God help us."

"I don't happen to think Devolution will serve at all," Yuill replied. "You know, the 'West Lothian Question'? How many Scottish MPs at Westminster? How many in Edinburgh? Who is authorised to vote for what? The proposed powers of reform in taxation are not flexible enough. And the position on North Sea oil revenues has not been made clear by the Devolutionists."

"So where do *you* stand, John?" asked Dr Renfrew.

"Well, listen, I think the jury's still out. The Tories will have to give way eventually, but if Labour win and push through Devolution I fear for the future. Control of our affairs, if they succeed, will still rest ultimately with Whitehall, and I don't judge that that's going to go down well with our people. Not in the longer term anyway. I believe we *should* have charge of things in Scotland."

"A bunch of kilted idiots in Edinburgh, with no experience at all. Couldn't govern themselves out of a paper bag! Is that what you want?" Cuthbertson made a disgusted gesture and turned to the bar to order another round.

"The transition could be bumpy," said Yuill quietly.

"What price the National Health Service in Scotland?" asked Renfrew of no-one in particular. "Of course I'm in private practice these days."

By the time Robert returned to his office, even the buffering of an excellent meal of roast venison, stilton and a couple of glasses of port was insufficient to dispel his general anxiety. There appeared to be no further bad news on the Home Front, although dealings remained extremely subdued. The conflicting views of his lunchtime cronies had not been at all reassuring. They were seemingly irreconcilable. It was perfectly sensible what John Yuill had said about the need for more control in Edinburgh. But if Devolution wouldn't secure that, or not to a sufficient degree at least, was separation from the UK the only answer. If it happened, could the Scots govern themselves satisfactorily? Or would they just go on arguing the toss interminably while the country went down the drain?

It was all hellish confusing. Nobody seemed to have enough facts on which to form a rational opinion. The whole thing was an absolute bloody nuisance! He had more than enough to worry about with the market. If only he could take a straightforward attitude like Muriel and just stick to it. But, really, that wasn't perhaps all that intelligent. The situation was fluid and the issues desperately important.

Thought of Muriel reminded him that she was in town today and was coming to the office about six for a lift home. She'd mentioned it the previous evening.

"Bob, a nice cheque came in this morning."

"Great. All welcome. From where?"

"Janey Smith. My notelets did a lot better than she'd anticipated. Had to print a second lot."

"Congratulations, my dear."

"Thanks, Bob. I'm taking Janey out to lunch in Glasgow to celebrate. I thought I'd do a bit of shopping after. Would it be all right if I came to you for a lift home about six? I hate driving in town."

"That'll be fine, Muriel. I'll look for you."

The two women drove in in Janey's car and parked in Blythswood Square. Their venue was the Glasgow Art Club, a fine

Victorian building with the style of Charles Rennie Mackintosh much in evidence. Muriel was the member. Her only regret was that she could no longer take her guest to the Society of Lady Artists, whose lovely old premises had been sold away years earlier. Daddy had somehow got her elected when she left the Art School: how proud she'd been.

Janey drank a gin and tonic, Muriel a fino sherry, San Patricio. Then they went to their table.

"This is very nice, Muriel, I must say."

"I think we've both earned it, Janey. Anyway, you've been very kind recently and I wanted to thank you. Now, what's on the menu?"

They ate their smoked salmon and veal escalopes companionably, chatting about Janey's business – some beautiful new craft lines in from Norway, the interest in pottery mugs seemed to have peaked – and speculating on whether they recognized any of the other diners. One very fat woman, clearly a professionally outré artist, wore on her head a tall contraption which looked like a crimson velvet lum-hat. Both of them started to giggle and had some difficulty regaining their composure. Janey particularly could not forbear to let out several loud snorts of suppressed laughter, which had people at nearby tables turning round.

"Oh dear!" said Muriel, wiping her eyes and taking a gulp of sparkling mineral water, "I haven't laughed so much for ages." She drank some more. "Know what Turgenev said, Janey?"

"No, what?"

"'It is possible to be original without being eccentric'."

"Wise old bird."

It wasn't until they were drinking coffee that Janey asked, "I suppose you saw the gory details about that political murder?"

Lines formed at the corners of Muriel's mouth. "Impossible to miss it. On TV too. I really do object to that sort of reporting at breakfast time, don't you?"

"Mmm." Janey put down her cup. "I read it in the *Glasgow Recorder*."

NOW YOU MUST DANCE

"Did you? I thought you took the *Herald*."

"I do, but the *Recorder* seems to be ahead of everyone else on this ghastly FSB business. I've started taking it as well as the *Herald*."

"I see," said Muriel.

"Of course I can't help seeing the articles by Willie Devine."

"Naturally."

"I realise your position, Muriel, and you know I completely sympathize. These media people have pretty slack ideas of personal behaviour, or so I'm told. I'm sorry that Gill's got involved with him, really I am, but I just have to say he writes brilliantly."

"Oh yes, he appears to have a facility with the pen, Janey. No great credit to him though. Either you have it or you don't. It's the *content* of his stuff, the drivel he retails about breaking up the UK, throwing Scotland to the tender mercies of the damned Socialists – that's what I object to. Strongly!"

"Yes." Janey finished her second cup of coffee and declined a refill. She glanced at her watch. "Again, I basically agree with you, Muriel, although I'm not quite sure he is a proper Labour supporter. Oh, sometimes I just don't know *what* to think! This constitutional thing is totally perplexing as far as I'm concerned. But *maybe* I'm coming round to the view that some change is more or less inevitable. Although, exactly what and when – well, please don't ask me!"

"I hadn't realized your political views were so mutable, Janey," said Muriel stiffly. "I'll get the bill," she signalled a waitress.

"Muriel, what I meant was ..."

"Oh, let's drop the subject, for goodness sake. I'm sick and tired of damned politics, Janey."

They left the club.

"So you don't need a lift back to Bearsden, Muriel?"

"No, I'm going to look round the shops, then go back with Bob. I'll see you to your car though, Janey. It's on my way."

They walked up to Blythswood Square, past the grand façade of the Royal Scottish Automobile Club. Two smartly dressed men came down the steps. One was James Ballantyne. He and Muriel

162

recognized one another.

"Mrs MacIntyre! What are you doing here?"

"Jamie, it's good to see you. We've been to the Art Club. This is my friend Janey Smith."

"Hello. This is Alec Beattie. A *very* important client. I've been lushing him up in there."

Laughter and handshaking all round.

Beattie said, "Are you Gill MacIntyre's mother?"

"I am."

"Charming. I've met her twice through Jamie, here."

"Have you?" said Muriel in some surprise.

"That was a while ago, Mrs MacIntyre." Jamie shook his head briefly. "Before she moved from Jordanhill."

There was an awkward silence.

"I must rush," said Janey.

"Yes, we too. Goodbye then." The men walked away.

"What a very pleasant young chap, Muriel,"

"Yes, isn't he?" said Muriel flatly.


Muriel did take a desultory stroll in one of the town's main shopping centres, but not for long. Soon she was in a taxi heading for Rubyvale Street. She'd been thinking of springing this surprise visit for some time.

No doubt turning up unannounced might annoy Gill, but Muriel couldn't face the possibility of being told by her daughter, by letter or on the phone, that her presence wasn't wanted. Of course it was no use pretending that her attitude to Willie Devine had changed in any way, and she wasn't going to try to give any such impression. That Gill was living with a man was bad enough but, well, all right, it was 1995, not 1945. However, Willie Devine was just not their type – dirt common if you had to say it. Even that she might have made an effort to live with, but the man was so absolutely bolshie on top of it.

This was not going to be easy, but Muriel MacIntyre missed her daughter. She knew her worth, her capacity for devotion, her reliability, her sheer genuineness, and was determined to re-establish at least a mutually respectful relationship, even if affection was, for the present anyway, not a possibility. Hopefully the man would not be in.

And so it proved. For a moment when she opened the door Gill was dumbstruck.

Muriel smiled. "May I come in, please?"

"Yes ... of course, Mum."

"Sorry to surprise you. I was in town and found I had some time to kill. Your father's taking me home at six. So I thought it's stupid not to run along to Partick. I reckoned, with luck, you'd be back from school. It was a spur of the moment idea."

"No, that's all right. Would you like some tea? I've got some digestive biscuits."

"That would be nice, dear."

She looked around while Gill prepared the tea. Much as she'd expected. Oppressively dull, cramped, antiquated. But it was clean. There was a hint of floor polish in the air, a pretty little vase of sweet-smelling freesias on a table by the window. The net curtains looked freshly washed. There were no pictures – Gill never had been particularly interested in such things – but a Colin Baxter calendar, with its breathtaking photographs of Scottish landscapes, did hang above the sideboard. If one *had* to live in this area and in this type of accommodation, Muriel supposed they'd made the best of it.

"How's Dad?"

"As ever, Gill. Fine."

"And Grandpa?"

"He's all right. He looked in at Muirlaw Drive the other day. I gather your Willie was out at Dungearie."

"That's right. Quite funny, really. They seem to have had a great old time together."

Muriel did not respond. Gill poured tea.

"Are you keeping well, Gill?"

"Never felt better, Mum."

"Fresh air would do you good. Why don't you come out to Bearsden to see us some time?"

"As a matter of fact, I was on the point of giving you a ring to arrange just that."

A quick smile came to Muriel's face, but then she peered more closely at her daughter.

"That's good to hear, Gill. Come any time. You must *know* we miss you, darling. Was there anything ... I mean, is there something you need from home? Or something you wanted to discuss?"

"No, nothing special really."

Muriel was no fool. She also possessed well-tuned powers of womanly intuition.

"I am your mother, Gill. I fed you at my breast, you know. Oh, you were a lovely wee girl!" She paused. "I hope you'd always feel you could confide in me. Little arguments shouldn't come between mother and daughter, should they, dear? We're both intelligent people, so we're bound to have slightly different views on some things. That's only natural."

No-one but Willie and Dr McCabe knew that Gill was pregnant. At three months it still didn't show. But Gill was increasingly aware of her condition, of nature's ineluctable processes at work. Indeed, sometimes it was hard to contain her mounting excitement. She did long to tell someone. The other day she'd almost blurted out the news to Cathie Lonie when she'd been going on about a newly born niece of hers in Dumfries. There sat her own mother, wearing Granny's beautiful amber beads, thoroughly competent to help her if anything were to go wrong, her child's grandmother, and she was obviously suing for a truce. Gill made her decision.

"Really, I wanted to come home just to see the old place. Maybe collect a few more of my books. There is something else though, Mum, seeing you're here now."

"What's that, dear?" Muriel held Gill's eye.

"I'm going to have a baby."

Muriel pursed her lips, but controlled any spontaneous reaction. "I see. I wondered."

"Wondered? What d'you mean, Mum?"

"I don't know. Something about the look of you perhaps. How long ... when are you due? Have you seen a doctor?"

"Yes, I have. Should be about mid-November I think."

"It is Willie's obviously?"

"Mum!"

"Sorry, sorry, Gill. It's just ... these days ... I can't keep up with attitudes nowadays. I'm sorry, Gill, I didn't mean that."

"OK. It's all right."

Muriel blew her nose daintily on a small pink, lace-edged handkerchief. "I have to ask, Gill. When do you plan to marry? I take it you're not thinking of ... you know ... well, abortion?"

"No abortion, Mum. No way. I *want* Willie's baby. We haven't really talked about marrying. He's been so busy. Anyway, he's not much in favour of the institution, as a general proposition."

The surface of Muriel's contrived calm exterior was beginning to crack. Spots of colour had appeared in her cheeks. "I'm not at all surprised that he has some peculiar notions about marriage, like most other things. But what about *you*, Gill? Your good name? Ours? And what about the baby's future?"

"Well, I'm afraid I regard this as a matter for Willie and me to decide. We're both adults, you know. The baby will have a good home and loving committed parents, which is more than lots of extremely conventionally brought-up kids get."

"But Gill, the baby! Is it fair? Your child, my grandchild incidentally, will be illegitimate! A *bastard*!" she shouted.

"Calm down, Mum. I hoped you wouldn't react like this. I told you, we haven't made any final decisions yet. But whatever we do in the end – if you don't like it, can't accept it, you can always disown me, can't you?"

"That's a rotten thing to say, Gill. You've changed. You're hard, cruel. And we all know who's responsible for that, don't we?"

"You don't like Willie, Mum. I can't help that. The awkward fact is I love him. I can see that my present situation is not easy for you, but has it occurred to you that I may also have difficulties, thinking about the future and so on? Self-doubts? I'd hoped for some comfort from you. More fool me." She was crying a little and got up to fetch a tissue.

Muriel shook her head in exasperation. "You're impossible!" she spat.

At this moment Willie arrived. He was as amazed as Gill had been to see Muriel.

"Oh, eh ... Mrs MacIntyre!"

"I just happened to be this way, so I dropped in."

"Aye, right. You've had some tea?"

"Gill very kindly made me some, thanks."

Gill took Willie's anorak. "Would you like a cup?"

"No thanks. I've been drinking cardboard coffee for the past two hours. In Sandy Black's room."

"That's Willie's Editor, Mum. Anything special?"

"Och, a bit of an argument about a piece I want him to print on the Royal Family. The cost to the people, their poor example etcetera etcetera."

"So you're against the monarchy I suppose?" said Muriel.

"Not on a personal level. I make it clear in my article that old Queenie has done her best, within the framework she inherited. And who could feel anything but friendly to the Queen Mum? Everybody's Granny. It's the rest I can't thole."

"Charles and Di?"

"The whole gang of them, Gill. Fergie, Margaret...the lot. See, ..."

"I'll have you know Princess Margaret is the Colonel-in-Chief of my father's regiment, the Royal Highland Fusiliers." Muriel stared at Willie. How she hated him! And yet, he seemed somehow to be considerably more civilized than the first time she'd met him. He'd got slimmer. He was well-shaven. His features were fine. He didn't *look* common. Almost refined, like ... what was she thinking of ... like, yes, sort of gypsy-like. Curly unparted black hair, good dark eyes, a curiously attractive crooked smile. Fleetingly, Muriel could almost see what had drawn Gill to the man. "So I'll ask you to speak respectfully about Princess Margaret."

"I don't want to be disrespectful to anyone. But, in my opinion, *unthinking* respect for royalty, whatever shenanigans they get up to, is plain stupid. I mean, what's the Royal Family done for Scotland?"

Muriel glanced at the ceiling. "They've set a standard which other countries envy. That's in general. As far as Scotland is concerned, I think we should be very grateful to them for spending their holidays here. I'm sure it helps bring in tourists."

"Standards? I'm not interested in making cheap points about all the sex scandals, but I can't see that their present-day example is particularly wonderful, or is likely to be so in the future. They're just human beings reacting to the moral environment in which they live. A weird environment of artificial privilege it is too. What's more important to me is that this exaggerated interest in the Royal Family distracts Scots from the issues that really do concern them – unemployment, poor health, emigration, for instance."

"They give people something to look up to."

Willie indicated total disagreement. "It makes me *squirm* to think of us as a nation of inferior bunnet-touching John Browns. If folks are curious, if they want a taste of the glamour, let them read about them as the Germans and Americans do in their glossy magazines. But not as *our* representatives."

Gill sat back. Let them slug it out. She just didn't want to participate.

Muriel was openly irritated. "So you'd take the SNP line and simple abolish the monarchy as far as Scotland is concerned? Right?"

"For your information the SNP do not take any such line. Their policy's that even if Scotland were independent, with our own Parliament and all that, the Queen and her successors would remain Head of State."

Muriel was honest enough to admit, "I didn't know that." But she wasn't going to be defeated. "But otherwise you agree with their objectives of course?"

"The Scottish National Party says a great number of absolutely sensible things. They're the only party without a Westminster presence to protect. But they also have some other ideas I can't go along with."

"Such as?"

"The right to vote for all citizens over sixteen for example. I'm not sure that there was any sense in lowering the voting age to eighteen, quite frankly. Another thing – the SNP's probably got some closet Devolutionists in its ranks. Just the same, if they can win enough votes to upset Labour's plans they'll get my support. Once the new Parliament is finally in being the Scottish voters will decide what the complexion of our Administration should be."

"Ninety-nine per cent Labour, obviously."

"I don't think anything's obvious in politics, Mrs MacIntyre. Circumstances can alter cases. And anyway, the Scottish Constitutional Convention is working on new voting systems to ensure that no one party dominates unreasonably."

"What party in all the wide world *do* you support then?"

"I don't. I'm an independent journalist. But if you forced me to put a label on it I suppose I might call it 'The Scottish Dignity, Economic Regeneration, Republican and Independence Party'."

"Och, really!" said Muriel, more furious by the minute. "That's just frivolous. Typical newspaper fence-sitting."

"It's not, Mum. Willie is being quite serious. If he showed partiality in his column, people would stop buying the *Recorder*. Or anyway they'd pay less attention to what he says."

Gill's voice brought Muriel back to the present. "Gill has told me about her condition. I'm not going to moralize, but can you tell me what you propose doing about it please? I am her mother."

For a moment Willie looked genuinely puzzled.

"I've told you, Mum. We haven't decided. Haven't discussed it properly yet. Nothing's planned."

"Yeah, that's about it," Willie agreed.

"Then I'm shocked at you! If you can spare a moment from your damned reporting, please *will* you discuss it? And, Gill, let us know, when it's convenient of course. Now I'm going. Your father will be delighted with my news."

Muriel left, her face flushed with anger.

They had a drink, orange juice for Gill, a whisky for Willie. There wasn't much to say about Muriel's visit: her reactions had been so predictable. For supper they ate finnan haddie and a lemon pie Gill had made. Afterwards they relaxed with television. About eight there was a loud knock. Gill answered.

"Is Willie Devine here?"

"Yes. Who ... ?"

Already two thickset men were pushing their way aggressively into the flat. They looked like labourers.

Willie stood up. "Who the hell d'you think ... ?"

"Shut it, fuck face! We want a word wi' you, Jimmie." The bigger of the men stabbed the air close to Willie's face with his finger, menacingly.

"OK. But tell us who you are."

"He's Jake Skilton, ma brither-in-law, an' Ah'm Allie Torrance. You're gonnae tell us whit we want tae know right noo or we'll bust yer balls!"

## ELEVEN

IT WAS BRUTALLY CLEAR these men meant business.

"Steady on, fella!" said Willie. "You're Wally's brother?"

"Aye."

"Listen, I'm hellish sorry about what happened. Wally was a friend of mine."

"OK. You'll ken whit we want then?"

"What is it, Allie?"

"Dinnae fuck aboot, Devine!"

The other man, ugly, balding and with a bad cast in his left eye, moved nearer.

"Tell me what it is you want to know. If I can help I'll ..."

"Whaur's fuckin' Danny Ramage?"

"I don't know. I've no idea."

"Don't gie us that shite! Ye ken fine, so y'do."

"No really. I haven't seen him for weeks."

Jake grunted. He was now standing behind Willie. "Lyin' cunt!"

"The guys doon the Argyle pub telt us you and Ramage wis chinas."

"No, not really. I've known him for a while right enough, but we weren't what you'd call actual friends."

Allie moved his head in a gesture of extreme frustration. "Listen, Devine, we didnae come up here tae play fuckin' gemmes. Tell us where this bastart Ramage is hidin' or you're gaun tae get somethin' ye'll no forget. *Right*?"

"All I know is he used to live out Bridgeton Cross way, but I never had his address."

"Aye, we've bin oot there. London Road. His fuckin' missus hasnae a clue. She telt us tae see you an' a'."

"I can't help you. Honest. He could be anywhere. London, over in Ireland, maybe even Amsterdam. In a situation like this you can never be ..."

"Aw, cut the fuckin' crap! We hivnae got a' night. Whit aboot *associates* of Ramage's?"

"I never knew any, Allie."

"You don't know nothin', do you, y' fuckin' lyin' bastart? Well, Ah don't believe you. Jake, get a haud o' him!"

Willie found his hands gripped and forced painfully up his back in a double half-nelson. As he involuntarily bent forward, Allie's knee came up smartly and crushed his testicles. Willie yelped with pain. A second knee-jerk sank into his midriff. Gill threw herself at the man, flailing with her fists. She was pushed back unceremoniously into a chair.

"Noo! Whaur's Ramage? Tell us or mebbe yer gaun tae get some mair persuadin'. *Whaur is he*?"

Willie managed to whisper, "I just don't know."

Allie lifted his eyebrows at Jake and Willie was released. As he collapsed to the floor, the boot of Allie crashed into his ribs.

"Ye lousy fuckin' bastart! Y'*ought* tae know. We'll mebbe be back."

The two aggrieved men left.

Gill, crying, somehow got Willie through on to the bed. She loosened his clothes and tried to comfort him. Paracetamol! She had some in the kitchen. They might help a bit. As she hurried to fetch the painkillers and a glass of water there was a quiet knock at the door. Hell! Who could it possibly be?

A worried Mrs Skelly stood in the doorway. "Is everything OK, hen? I couldnae help hearin' scufflin' like. An' Willie shoutin'."

"I think he's all right, thanks. It was a bit of a fight about something, Mrs Skelly."

"You greetin', Gill?"

"I'm OK. Really."

"Give Mr Devine my best then. He shouldnae be fechtin' at his age, mind. No wi' big buggers like yon onywey. I seen them gangin' oot the close."

Gill did what she could for Willie. He was in pain, but it was containable. Just. After an hour or so she made him drink a cup of milky sweet tea and he took some more tablets. Eventually he fell asleep. Much later a worried Gill also slipped into unconsciousness.

Near three she was awakened by the sound of muffled weeping. Willie's face was half under the duvet. She put her mouth close to his ear.

"What is it, darling? Is the pain bad?"

He gave a hard sob which went to her heart.

"No, it's not that. It's everything!"

"What d'you mean?"

"Och, Gill, I just don't know." He whimpered miserably.

She knelt beside him, bent down and kissed his forehead tenderly. "You're bound to be upset, Willie, after tonight. It was horrible."

His anguish came tumbling out. "Maybe that finally got me thinking. Can my stand be justified? I mean, look at the suffering, Gill. Two men dead, one hellishly tortured first, two men in jail, for most of their lives probably. Families devastated. A man on the run being hunted down for execution if he's caught. What's next? Or who's next? Are we looking at the Irish tit-for-tat pattern starting in Scotland? Could things escalate like that? Oh God ... !"

He was crying again and shaking. Gill's protective instincts rose within her. This was her lover and the father of her baby. She simply would not *let* him slide into a breakdown. He *mustn't* doubt himself. She lay down and put her arms round him.

"Willie, you mustn't doubt yourself. None of those awful things have been your fault. Your stand is quite clear and honest. You've nothing, nothing at all to be ashamed of. If others make mistakes, or betray each other, or behave like thugs, you're not to blame, my darling man. You're the brave one, not them."

"I don't know, Gill. I can't get the faces of those poor wee Hosseins out of my mind. And Hamish MacCorquodale too. He's living in mental *agony*, and probably fear. Anyway, what about your own family? Willie Devine and his political views haven't exactly brought joy and unity, have they?"

"Don't worry about that, Willie. Their happiness is their affair. All I know is that I love you, more than anything, I believe in you, and you make *me* very happy."

This passionate assurance of faith and support brought more tears from the exhausted man. However, after a few more tablets and another cup of warm tea he was deep in sleep. Gill listened in the dark to his even breathing with something like proprietorial satisfaction, but from time to time a deeply troubling anxiety for the future caused her to frown.

Muriel had managed to withhold her bombshell until Robert and she were safely home. He'd talked about the market upset and his conversation with Philip Cherrington in the City. She'd described her lunch with Janey Smith at the Art Club and running into young Jamie Ballantyne.

When they were finally indoors at Muirlaw Drive, coats off and lights switched on, she said, "You'd have noticed I didn't do any shopping this afternoon, Bob?"

"Oh, eh ... as a matter of fact, Muriel, actually ..."

"No, I suppose you wouldn't." She was already marginally irritated, and they'd hardly *started* to talk! She closed her eyes briefly. "I went somewhere else."

"Uh-huh? A gallery? An exhibition?"

"I went to Partick."

Robert made an exaggerated nod of comprehension. "I see. To Gill." He knew this was going to lead to conflict. It was written all over Muriel's face. "Hang on a minute, dear, while I get a whisky. Then I'll hear all about it. Anything for you?"

"No thanks," she replied, irritated further as she recognized the characteristic kick for touch.

Robert had his glass well-charged. "Well, how was Gill? Is she fit?"

"Blossoming. In a way."

"Good, good. And Willie? He's getting a bit famous, I think."

"Oh I don't doubt that. The drivel he writes is absolutely up the street of the bolshie ..."

"All right, Muriel, all right. Tell me about Gill."

Muriel's carapace of even temper was again disintegrating. "If I hadn't been rudely interrupted, I was coming to Gill. For your parental information, everything is decidedly *not* all right."

Robert sighed. "What's wrong? Is she unwell?"

This was it. If this didn't shake him into action, nothing would, she thought. "Gill's pregnant."

"*Pregnant*?"

"That's what I said."

"Did she tell you herself?"

"D'you think I'd have put it that way if I was just guessing?"

"No, no, I suppose not." Robert took a quick mouthful of whisky and water. "How long till ... ?"

"Mid-November is the due date, I understand."

"Oh well then, they'll marry soon."

"Not if Mr Devine has anything to do with it. He doesn't believe in such silly old-fashioned institutions."

"Did he say that?"

"Certainly."

"And Gill? What is she saying?"

"She'll go along with whatever he wants. Claims she shares his outlook."

"I see," said Robert, apparently accepting the situation.

Muriel exploded. "What d'you *mean*, Bob? You 'see'? Surely you can't put up with this insult?"

Robert took another gulp of whisky. Oh God! Once more Muriel was going to push him into a corner. He felt his heartbeat quickening. "I don't see it as an insult."

"Wilfully making us grandparents to an illegitimate child? Not an insult?"

"Well, it has to be their decision whether to marry or not, I suppose. In the end anyway. We can't insist, can we, Muriel?"

"We can have a damned good try! We at least are decent people with decent standards, Robert, I hope?"

"Yes, of course, Muriel. I know that. I wish everyone would behave normally, rationally. But they don't. And times are changing, I ..."

"You're going to give in, aren't you? Put up no fight. Is that your reaction to all this?"

"I resent that remark, Muriel. It's inappropriate in any case. You don't 'fight' in a situation like this. Maybe try to persuade, not fight."

"So we let our daughter live her life out in the slums breeding bastard children for an unprincipled layabout?"

Robert drained his glass. "For God's sake, Muriel! Control yourself. Whatever else Willie Devine may be, he's neither unprincipled nor a layabout."

"Oh, so now you're going to stick up for the rotten beggar! That's rich. I was treated this afternoon to another dose of his so-called principles. He wants to do away with the Queen, the monarchy, and turn Scotland into some kind of leftist republic. As if the whole Royal Family and the framework they provide didn't matter *that much*." She snapped her fingers.

"A bit extreme, but I have to admit I'm not much enamoured of them myself these days. In this day and age they have to behave. If they can't, maybe they'd be better pensioned off."

"Och, it's impossible to talk to you!"

"Muriel, I wonder if you realise just how difficult it's become to talk to *you*?"

"Maybe you'd better pension me off."

Muriel's joke died in the telling. There was a hiatus while Robert poured himself a second whisky.

"Will they stay on where they are?" he enquired.

"Don't ask me. Anyway, what's the point in discussing it with you? It's obvious you're going to take the coward's way out, as usual, and do nothing at all."

Robert bridled. "Take that back, Muriel!"

"The truth hurts, doesn't it Bob?"

He shouted, "If I thought it would be wise to interfere I'd go down to see Gill, and Willie, straight away. But I don't. They're both grown-up people with their own lives and their own ideas. If they want to marry, they will. Naturally I hope they will. But I'm not going to barge in like you, stamping about like a rogue elephant!"

"Elephant?" questioned Muriel, her eyebrows arched in surprise.

"Yes, a damned great clumsy elephant!" Robert was still shouting. "To try to lay down the law like that would be the surest way to alienate Gill finally. And I happen to *love* both my daughters."

"Unlike me, I suppose?"

"Ach, the only person you love, Muriel, is yourself. Unless everyone fits neatly into a mould of your designing, one that will flatter you of course, they're unacceptable. I consider your attitudes contemptible, narrow-minded."

"Well!" said Muriel, nonplussed for a moment.

Robert was fired up. "It's not just this business of Gill and Willie Devine. Your opinions about the country's political future – you're impossibly rigid."

She recovered her voice. "Am I now? What's your up-to-date view then? Throw everything out with the bath water, I suppose? Monarchy, educational excellence, morality. Tax the well-off till they're brought down to the common denominator of those who've either no talent or are just plain idle. Is that what you'd like to see come about?"

Robert took a long drink. "We just don't agree on anything, do we, Muriel? I sometimes wonder if we ever did. I don't know what lies ahead politically in Scotland. I don't even pretend to have a strong, informed opinion about what I think will be best. I wish I did. But I do know it's useless going on blindly as you do. It's about as intelligent as Canute. But you won't change."

"No, *I certainly won't!*"

"Exactly."

An oppressive silence developed between them.

At length Muriel said, "Are we going to discuss Gill any more then?"

"I can't think of anything I want to discuss with you, Muriel," said Robert with deliberation.

It was as absolute a rejection as a slap in the face and Muriel understood it. Suddenly she felt a prompting of fear.

"I'd better go and see what I can find for supper. Pasta all right?"

"No supper for me. I'm going out."

"When will you be back, Bob?"

"I don't know. Late. Put some pyjamas in the spare room, if you will."

He left the house. With rising dismay, Muriel heard the Jaguar's silky engine fade into the distance.


Robert parked about a hundred yards from the block of flats in Kelvinside where Lilias Watson, his long-time secretary, lived. He walked quickly to the building and up to the third floor.

"Mr MacIntyre! What's happened? Come in."

"I just wanted to see you, Lilias dear."

"Lovely, but unexpected! Are you hungry? I've a tiny fish pie in the oven. Not much for two, but you could have some cheese after. An apple?"

"That'll be grand, Lilias."

"Right. Can I get you a whisky?"

"Better not. I've had a couple already and I'll have to drive back. Just come here and let me kiss you."

"We're amorous tonight are we?" she said, smiling and quickly melting into his open arms.

"Not quite like that, Lilias darling. I just need to love you, badly. It's not a happy night."

She was all unfeigned consternation. "What is it, Bob? The children? Gill, is it? Anything at the office? The Scottish shares fall?

178

Och, I'm sorry you're unhappy."

He hugged her tightly and spoke above her head. "No, it's none of those. Not directly anyway. It's the usual."

"Muriel. Has she been going on again?"

"Yes, you could say that, Lilias."

Over their small meal together he outlined the elements of his latest row with his wife. Lilias was familiar with the pattern. She'd been a counsellor in the matter for several years now.

"It strikes me that Gill's situation is bringing a number of issues between you to a head, Bob."

"That's perfectly true. Trouble is it's getting rather obvious we're no longer compatible. There's a limit to what diplomatics can achieve, in the long run."

Lilias was a generous-hearted woman. Above all, that was what Robert loved in her. "Maybe Gill will decide to get married after all. Then at least Muriel's sense of the conventions would be placated. Perhaps things'll settle down again, Bob dear." She wrinkled her nose encouragingly.

"God, Lilias! What would I do without you?" said Robert.

They ate quickly. She put on a CD of Tchaikovsky ballet music, then made coffee. Robert relaxed for the first time that day. He signalled to her to join him on the couch. Fifteen minutes later they were in Lilias's bed, embracing and hungrily running their hands up and down one another's backs.

Lilias was a well-fleshed woman of forty-four. The combination of her feminine amplitudes, her eager sexuality and her tender solicitude for his pleasure never failed to rouse him. They made practised, utterly satisfying love.

As their passion subsided she whispered, "That was wonderful, Bob. Thank you."

He replied, "Thank *you* my darling. I love you very much."

They lay silent for a while. During that time Robert came to a decision. Dressed again and preparing to drive back to Bearsden, he kissed Lilias gently, then said, "I don't think I can go on with Muriel. If I arrange to be free of her, would you have me, Lilias?"

"Oh Bob!" she responded immediately, "what about the children? I mean ... ?"

"They're grown-up, Lilias, out in the world making their own lives, their own decisions. I'll always do what I can for them of course, but my direct responsibility as a father, for their welfare and so on, has gone."

"Yes, I suppose that's right."

"Well?"

"Bob, you *know* how much I love you and admire you. Of *course* I'd have you as my husband. I can't think of anything that would make me happier. I promise I'd try my best to be a good wife if you really want me in that capacity."

She was so earnest, such a lovable woman. Her eyes were shining. Bob gave her a final kiss. "Then leave it to me," he said. Oh, how he longed for uncritical, spontaneous love.

Despite many deep-seated aches in his body, Willie got up late in the morning after the visit by Wally Torrance's avengers. At the office he wrote a piece making a powerful plea for peaceful constitutional change. Without mentioning names, he referred to reprisal attacks and ruthless manhunts as the likely sequel to any further terrorist incidents which might occur if political initiatives did not happen soon. He warned against the avoidable tragedy of an IRA-type tit-for-tat escalation in Scotland. In some other newspapers an increasing trend towards a similar line was detectable.

"The maddening thing is," Willie pointed out to Gill, "that general editorial recommendations are for Labour's Devolution package."

"And you don't think that will be enough to quieten potential troublemakers?"

"It probably would, for a while. Maybe there wouldn't be any outbreaks of violence while a Devolved Assembly got going. But I'm looking farther ahead, to the frustrations of still ultimately being controlled by Westminster. Still being in a second class relationship. Still being under a discredited monarchy. Still thirled to a crazily expensive defense policy. That's Labour's Devolution!"

"Yes, I understand, Willie. What Scotland needs is Independence as a member of the EC in her own right."

"That's what I'll keep banging on about till I drop, Gill." He smiled. "Mind you, I'm not saying we wouldn't have our arguments with Brussels, just as happens now. But Scotland ought to be able to fight her own corner. Like, say, the Danes. Fishing, offshore oil taxation. Things which are really important here."

Willie kept working but the strain was telling. He slept badly. Eventually he took Gill's advice and went to see Dr McCabe about a prescription for sleeping pills.

On the way his bus was halted for a time by some roadworks. Willie laid his paper down and gazed at a group of teenagers below, standing outside a fast food dispensary. Obviously unemployed, they gave the appearance of a weirdly-dressed, self-contained unit. Passers-by carefully avoided them.

Two of the young men sported glowing primary-coloured 'mohican' cockscombs, the girls' heads were shaven and, in one case, strangely tattooed. They wore a motley mixture of metal-studded leather jackets and unclean-looking blue jean material. All displayed cheap silver earrings, some several per ear, and a particularly tall girl had had her septum pierced to accommodate another.

Willie watched the tall girl. He noticed that her brief leather skirt revealed long, rather shapeless, thin white legs. These terminated in bright yellow-laced ugly boots, 'Doc Marten's'. Then he noticed the plentiful freckles on her face. Suddenly the outlandish gear seemed to fade away and there was Mina, his big sister of long ago, playing peevers with her friends while he whipped his peerie. Red-haired Mina had used to get so angry with her freckles.

A great wave of affection for the girl swept through Willie, an affection which quickly became a deeper compassion for the whole wayward group. They couldn't all be wasters, surely? Oh, there'd always be a number of workshy characters, of course there would. And undoubtedly these youngsters would not have escaped the disorientating effects of early exposure to solvent abuse and other drugs. (May the devilish dealers who ensnare eager youth roast in eternal torment! thought Willie – crucifixion would be too good.) And no doubt they'd left the school system poorly educated, virtually illiterate.

But the fact was that there was no work for them. Probably their parents, if they had the luck of two parents, were likewise permanently on the dole. Was it surprising that these kids took refuge from society, which seemed implacably hostile to them, in extreme behaviour and the group solidarity of similarly victimised individuals? If they could not aspire to personal dignity, at least this type of separateness conferred a certain sense of identity, however spurious. And, marginalized as they were, it was self-deluding to expect them to take the same attitude to crime – robbery, muggings, prostitution – as did stable citizens.

Willie looked again at the youngsters. He imagined their idle days. Quite apart from probable potentially dangerous drug abuse, they were all polluted people. Never mind the diesel fume-heavy atmosphere of the Partick streets, their innards had to contend with a regular diet of fat-sodden convenience foods; their unbrushed teeth were rotting from an unending bombardment of Coca Cola and Irn Bru; their lungs were fighting a losing battle with nicotine tar – didn't Willie know all about that?; their eyes absorbed a daily quota of mind-deadening TV game shows and soap operas; their ears received through Walkman plugs a constant stream of deafening cacophonous pop music trash.

The bus moved on. Willie knew very well that a change in Scotland's constitutional status, however radical, was not going to do away with this distressing social underclass, or perhaps more accurately described, this growing population of disaffected social outcasts. It was a widespread world problem owing something to the electronic revolution, the decline of religiously-based moral values and a failure of leadership. Nevertheless, efforts *must* be made to improve educational standards and to find employment for the country's youth.

He was convinced that most young people only needed a realistic chance, a genuine hope of escaping the social welfare poverty trap, to be willing to join the productive community as responsible citizens. If these areas were firmly under Scotland's control, immediate plans, tailored to the country's specific needs, could be put into action. The very fact that responsibility rested right here would be salutary. Hard-core spongers would be rounded on more readily as letting the side down. And the eternal cop-out of blaming the government, meaning the distant faceless English mandarins in Westminster and Whitehall, that malevolent administration bent on punishing Scotland for not voting for them – that cop-out would no longer be available.

Willie was under no delusions about the magnitude of social engineering problems inherent in late twentieth century society: he simply believed, passionately, that Independence for Scotland within the EC framework would enable an active hands-on attack to be mounted on these problems, without the constant looking over the shoulder and the possibilities for excuse inseparable from the present, outdated political yoking with England. Willie had strong faith in his countrymen's and countrywomen's good sense and capabilities, once given the opportunity to act freely, to innovate.

As he sat in Dr McCabe's waiting room he was too preoccupied mentally to read the dog-eared *Antique Collector* magazine which he had picked up from the central table.

By the second post an unexpected letter came to Gill. She recognized her mother's forwarding hand but not that of the originator. The postmark was Edinburgh. Curiously, she slit the envelope.

*Dear Gill,*
*I hope you won't mind my writing to you but I don't see how else to communicate. James Ballantyne told me you'd left*

*your previous address and he didn't know where you were now living. So he gave me your parents' house and I hope this will be safely sent on.*

*I gather James and Charlotte Ch-P are something of 'a unit' these days and so I felt free to contact you.*

*The thing is, Gill, I admired you very much when we met at that dinner party. You seemed to me not only to be a most attractive person but also to be level-headed and interested in things which interest me, such as Scotland's political future – unlike some I could mention who were present that night!*

*I feel we could enjoy one another's company and would like so much to take you out to supper one evening if you're free. As you can see, I'm now back in the Edinburgh office (the property market's had a burst of activity), but it will be easy for me to come through any time if you're willing.*

*Let me know what you think.*

*Meantime, fond regards and best wishes,*

*Guy Beaumont*

Gill put the letter back in its envelope and slipped it into her personal writing case. She smiled to herself. Oh well, it was good to know that one could still make an impression! She'd think about it and maybe mention it to Willie. Nearly four – he should be back quite soon. In fact it was six before Willie returned: he'd dropped into the Argyle on the way home.

The scene was much as ever. Through the thick atmosphere the frieze of gesticulating men along the bar looked unchanged, eternal almost. An undulating susuration of muttering and grunting was punctuated by earnest head-wagging and emphatic finger stabbing.

"Hullo, Willie!"

A diminutive man in cap, suit jacket, jeans and trainers detached himself from the crowd and advanced with arm extended. It was Jumpie MacPherson, a drouthy ex-soldier credited with some youthful boxing victories at bantamweight. Willie knew him slightly.

"Hi, Jumpie."

"How're ye daein', Willie?"

"All right."

"That's gude, Willie. Ah'm hivin' a helluva bad run the noo. Nae job, the wife needin' maist o' ma unemployment fur the kids an' that – know whit Ah mean, Willie?"

"Aye, OK, Jumpie. What'll it be?"

"Hauf an' a hauf, Willie, if ye can manage it, like?"

"Right." He called the barman.

"Aw look! Y're a right gentleman, Willie, So y'are. Ah fuckin' *appreciate* it. Do the same fer you wan day, when ma ship comes in. Naw, really!"

They toasted one another's health. Willie noticed the frayed teeshirt under Jumpie's irredeemably faded blue pinstripe jacket: 'Glasgow's Miles Better', it proclaimed – relic slogan from a large scale civic promotion ten years earlier.

"Well now, Jumpie, I've not been in for a bit, what with one thing and another. Fill me in on what's been happening." Willie was well aware of the little man's reputation for gossiping.

"Oh, aye, weel ... 'Course the big item wis Wally's murder. The regulars wis fuckin' angry. But whit can they dae? Nothin'. Leave it tae the polis, that's whit Ah keep tellin' them."

"A terrible business. You'd wonder how Wally's family took it, Jumpie, wouldn't you?"

"Aye weel, as a matter of fact ... " He dropped his voice, his eyes darting about. "Wan o' Wally's brithers *did* come in, wi' anither guy, askin' a' aboot Danny Ramage an' that. Naebody could tell them onything. Ramage's never been a regular in the Argyle. Some o' the boys *do* know him, but no intimate, like. He disnae belang tae Partick furby."

Willie took his time, then said, "It's hard to understand why Wally would grass, isn't it, Jumpie? I mean, irrespective of his own views."

"Ah think there's an answer tae that, Willie." He looked down pointedly at his empty whisky glass.

"Would you care for another dram, Jumpie?"

"That's fuckin' kind o' you, Willie. Ah'll no forget it. Thanks, aye."

A second time they toasted one another.

"So you were saying, Jumpie, about Wally?"

"Yeah, that's right ... aye ... Wan o' the boys put that actual question tae yon Allie – that wis whit Wally's brither ca'd hissel, Willie."

"And?"

"Allie telt us Wally got intae some bad trouble when he was young. Seems he hud a lousy record a'ready, so he wis fur the high jump. But the polis let him aff on condition he turned informer fur them, the bastarts. An' he's hud t'dae it ever since."

"I see."

"Allie said it was jist wee crimes he telt them about – y'know, thievin', sellin' goods on an' that kinna stuff. Chat he picked up at the bar."

"This business was in a different category, Jumpie."

"Aye, Willie, it wis. That's true enough."

"Did they say if Wally was paid for information?"

"No. Mebbe he wis an' mebbe he wisnae. Christ knows. Naebody hud the bottle tae ask that Allie. He wis a big evil bastart, Willie, ken?"

Willie nodded. Slowly, as if speaking to himself, he said, "You'd wonder how the killers got on to Wally. How the hell they worked it out?"

Jumpie shuffled closer. "Whit Ah heard wis that two o' Ramage's men, confederates like, showed up ootside at closin' time. They done over thon Shug Smith."

"Shug? Wally's assistant?"

"Aye. Part-timer. See, Wally wis aff that night. God knows how they suspected. Mind you, Ah'd believe onything, so Ah would ... 'Course, Wally an' Shug wis gey close ... but that disnae explain it. Naw, there has tae be anither."

"What d'you mean, Jumpie?"

The little man screwed up his nose. "It could easy of bin a bent fuckin' sodjer fingered Wally. Them polis is corrupt tae their marrows, Willie. That's ma personal theory onyweys."

They finished their drinks and Willie left Jumpie to look for further hospitality elsewhere. Gill would be waiting for him. He stepped outside.

"Willie! Long time no see."

It was Tommy Bell.

"Tommy, I thought you'd moved?"

"Aye, we're out by Victoria Park now. Are you fit for a dram?"

"Thanks, Tommy, but I'm due home."

"Too bad. I thought I'd just have one in the Argyle for old time's sake. Not many of us left, Willie, eh?"

"The last couple of months have been unbelievable, Tommy."

"Aye indeed. Still, life goes on for some of us. I've just been up at the BBC seeing about a TV adaptation of 'Walls'."

"Congratulations, Tommy."

"Thanks. They seem keen."

Willie had no further comment to offer. Bell sensed it.

"I looked for our old teuchter friend at Queen Margaret Drive."

"Hamish? How is he?"

"He's gone. Fired."

"Why? What happened?"

"His erstwhile secretary bird indicated that the powers that be got wind of Mr MacCorquodale's political entanglements and didn't like it. One hour to clear his desk evidently."

"Poor devil! He was so keen on that Gaelic history series he was working on too."

"This wee girl said he was shattered. Big binge of the waterworks right there in the office. She started crying herself, just telling me."

"Oh hell. Where is he?"

"She thought he'd buggered off back to Stornoway. Apparently he said something to her about a possible opening in Canadian television."

Sadly Willie hurried to Rubyvale Street. He told Gill about Hamish's dismissal and also about Jumpie MacPherson's revelation.

She showed him Guy Beaumont's letter.

"You go, Gill. Take a dinner off old Guy. His political heart's in the right place by the sound of it. Make him an ally. Maybe he'll be useful one day. Anyhow, you should enjoy yourself and keep in touch with the world."

"All right, Willie. I'll do that. Tell me, did you see the doctor?"

"Yes. The sleeping pills are right here." He pulled a small bottle out of his pocket. "I got my money's worth. I told her about my aches and actually had a major coughing fit in Dr McCabe's room!"

"Oh Willie!"

"Net result, I've been up to the Western Infirmary this afternoon for x-rays. Took ages." He laughed as casually as he could manage.

That night Willie slept for a straight ten hours, but Gill lay awake nagged by anxiety. At lunchtime next day she had just posted a reply to Guy Beaumont when Willie rang her at school.

"Gill, Dr McCabe's had a message from the hospital. They want me to go in again today, now in fact."

Gill's heart was racing. "Willie darling, what's wrong?"

"She wouldn't say. Just mentioned something about a need for further tests. Try not to worry, sweetheart."

He sent her a kiss down the line.

## TWELVE

THE EVENING AFTER their row over Gill Robert confronted Muriel.

"I have no intention of putting up with another of your screaming exhibitions," he said. "Let's try to keep this on a civilized level, shall we?"

"Just tell me what you want to say, Bob."

"Right. I'm telling you, Muriel, that our marriage is over. There's no longer any joy in it for either of us. We just don't agree on anything, whether it's the children or politics or ... oh, I don't know what."

"That's your opinion."

"No, it's not! It's bloody obvious. You know it, Muriel. If you *haven't* recognized the sheer bankruptcy of our situation then you're an even bigger fool than I thought."

"Who's screaming now, Bob?"

"Och, for God's sake, Muriel! Face it – we're done. We've brought the children up properly and there's now no reason to stay together except for appearances."

"What about vows?"

"I suggest we leave vows, conjugal rights and the rest of it out of the picture." There was no response. "I've been to see Angus Spence today."

"The lawyer? You mean ..." Tears welled in Muriel's eyes. "You really mean divorce?"

"I do, Muriel. And you can stow the tears. It's only self-pity. Too late, Muriel. It's far too late. This has been coming for years but you've been too cocksure of yourself and your damned inflexible opinions to wish to do anything about it."

"Bob ... couldn't we ... ?"

"No. I've patched things up once too often. If you need it spelled out, Muriel, the worm has turned at last."

She dabbed her eyes. "So you've got some kind of proposal, have you?"

"Yes. Now listen carefully, Muriel. This is what I suggest we do. Spence thinks it's fair and workable."

"Go on."

"We part as soon as the necessary agreement is drawn up and signed by us both. A legal separation. Formalization of a decree takes a while, as you know." He took a deep breath, a look of resignation on his face. "I want to be generous, so you can have the house and contents. Of course you could sell it for a bonny penny if you wanted to move into, say, a small flat. I'll make over an agreed quantity of fourteen percent corporate bonds. You have your father's annuity and substantial expectations from him in due course, so you'll be perfectly comfortable."

"Very neat, Bob. You've got it all mapped out, haven't you?"

Suddenly suppressed anger erupted. "You miserable cold bitch! I'm doing my damnedest to provide for you, making sacrifices of hard-earned cash, and all you can do is sneer. To hell with you, Muriel! Who d'you think you are anyway? You never did a hand's turn all your life."

Crying now with vexation and apprehension, Muriel shouted back, "That's a rotten thing to say, Bob! I never had a *chance* to work! You didn't let me!"

He cradled his forehead with his right palm, then looked up. "It's just not going to do any good chucking recriminations at one another, Muriel, whether justified or not. We've reached the end of the line."

She sniffed and briefly compressed her lips, hard. Staring intently at him she asked, "There wouldn't by any chance be somebody else? I've often wondered. Those convenient conferences. Might you ... ?"

"Muriel! I just don't want to listen to you any more. I'm an easy-going person who doesn't like rows, upsets. But you've taken advantage of me for years. I've felt humiliated sometimes in company. It may be that in your arrogance you've stopped realizing how you behave. I don't know. But I do know that the last few years have been miserable as far as I'm concerned. And your attitude over Willie Devine has been the last straw. I want out, *now*."

"You drag him up? A man who's ruining our daughter's life and trying to smash everything we believe in?"

"There you are, you see. Gill wants Willie and he's a decent chap doing an interesting job. I don't have to accept everything he says about politics and so on. But ..."

"I don't think you know *what* your politics are."

"I admit it. I simply don't know which path Scotland should take. I'm totally confused at the minute."

"Well, I'm not. There's absolutely no need to change ..."

"I'm *not* getting into all that again Muriel! We're separating, with a written agreement to divorce as soon as the law permits. Do you accept the terms I've outlined?"

"I don't seem to have any option."

"So I'll instruct Spence to draw up the papers?"

"I suppose so." She sat looking forlorn. "I've got some liver. D'you want me to fry it or are you going out?"


Next morning Muriel drove out to Dungearie. Mrs Campbell admitted her.

"Come away in, Mrs MacIntyre! The Major will be that glad tae see you. Beautiful day, isn't it? I love the early summer. Magic."

Major Colquhoun showed no surprise at his daughter's news. However, he did offer her a quick and genuine sympathy.

"I'm so sorry, my dear. This kind of thing is painful. You must be suffering."

"Yes, Daddy, it's awful. I feel so angry at Bob. He was so damned *clinical* about it when he told me."

"Maybe that's better than dreeing things out?"

"Oh I suppose so."

"Did Bob ... I mean, what did he actually say about his reasons?"

"That we don't agree about much these days and he hates arguments. He seems to think I'm 'arrogant and inflexible'. Evidently my political attitudes – respecting the Queen and wanting to keep up standards in general – are all out of date. Although Bob himself doesn't seem to have *any* clear opinions, by the way. Oh, and I'm at fault for not falling over backwards to welcome Willie Devine into the bosom of our family." Muriel checked herself. "I know you find Willie an interesting character, Daddy, but I think you know what I mean?"

"Yes, I understand, Muriel. I do understand. You're my own wee dochter, you know." He put his arm round her shoulders and kissed her on the cheek.

Muriel broke down. "Oh, Daddy, Daddy! I'm so miserable and lost." She grasped his tweed jacket. "It's true Bob and I have not been getting on. Maybe we'll be better apart now the girls have gone. But it's the reasons I can't cope with." She sobbed.

"There now, Muriel," said the Major softly. "There, there, darling. Don't cry now."

"I'm sure I'm right not to want our country to become some horrible socialist mess. No private schools, killing taxation on people like us, your 'Cloth Cap Brigade' lording it, Butlin's camps everywhere! Imagine!" She reached into her bag for a tissue.

To Muriel's annoyance her father laughed loudly. "Oh dear, Muriel! That last one's a vision of hell, if ever there was! But I don't think the present Labour leaders would recognize your forecast. And bear in mind that most of them are Scots anyway."

"Traitors!" she spat, drying her eyes.

Muriel's tears had not lasted long. At the Major's prompting she explained the proposed financial settlement.

"I'd say Bob's being very fair indeed, Muriel. And if there's any problem in the future you know I'd always help you. It's final then? You don't think you could yet compose your differences?"

"No, I'm afraid Bob's made up his mind. I know him. He'll

swither for ages, but when he does decide on something he's impossible to shift."

"I see. Well, if there's no hope I think you'd better accept and turn the page." The door opened. "Ah ... Margaret, fine. Muriel, you'd like a cup of coffee and a piece of Margaret's delicious shortbread I'm sure?"

"Yes, Daddy, I would."

The Major enquired about Gill.

"That was the thing that eventually brought all this to a head. Prepare yourself for a shock, Daddy."

"Shock? Dearie me, I can do without those at my age, Muriel. *Your* news is enough for one day."

"I'm sorry but I have to tell you that Gill is going to have a baby by Mr Devine, but he does not intend to marry her."

For a moment Major Colquhoun was simply puzzled. Such a pattern of behaviour did not tally with any precedents in his experience that he could think of. He asked, "But what does Gill say? They're still together, I take it?"

"That's the damnable part of it, Daddy. She seems quite untroubled at the prospect."

"They've no plans at all?"

"Neither to get rid of the child by abortion or adoption, nor to get married."

"Good Lord!" said the Major. Then, collecting his thoughts, he enquired, "How did you first hear this? Did Gill ring you up?"

"I went to see them in Partick."

"Did you? And what did you say to them?"

"Told them to start planning *immediately*, that the Colquhouns and the MacIntyres were not accustomed to breeding bastard children. I gave *him* a real flea in his ear, I can tell you."

He looked at Muriel's flushed face, her still pink eyes. She'd always been a determined child, intent on getting her own way. If only there'd been siblings, it might have softened her. But that had not been the way of it. "Perhaps I'll try to see Gill soon," he said quietly. "But the young folks do have different ideas about these things from our day. I am aware of that, Muriel."

Guy Beaumont replied by return post that he'd be in Glasgow the following Thursday and had booked a table at the Rogano Restaurant. He hoped it wasn't too old-fashioned a venue for Gill's taste but expected it would be quiet so that they could talk.

The famous Art Deco surroundings were indeed discreet and Gill found herself quite excited as she entered. Guy was downstairs waiting for her. He rose and shook her hand.

"Ah, hello, Gill! It's very nice to see you again."

"Yes, Guy. Thanks for your letters." She sat down.

"Apéritif? Martini? G & T?"

"I'm off the booze actually. Just a mineral water, thanks." Would the conversation give her a chance to tell Guy? At the least she simply must explain about living with Willie.

"Oh, OK." He summoned a waitress, a pale-skinned girl with very red lips and a period, Katherine Mansfield hair style. "You're well, Gill, I hope?"

"Fine, yes."

They studied menus and ordered.

"How's teaching?"

"Slightly boring. Too much paperwork. But I enjoy the kids. You?"

"Edinburgh's a bit stuffy, I find, after Glasgow. Still, there's the Festival in a couple of months."

"You're busier with the estate selling?"

"That was a bit of a false alarm, Gill. Interest rates popped up and killed the market stone dead. Actually, I'm writing a novel. Takes up a lot of my time."

"Really? What's it about?"

"Well ... it's a bit autobiographical, I must admit. But then, first novels invariably are."

"Well done all the same, Guy. Stick at it."

"Yes, I will, thanks, Gill." He smiled at her with open gratitude for the encouragement.

Their drinks arrived.

"Slàinte-mhah!" said Gill.

"What? Oh, of course. Cheers, and 'Bon Appetit'!"

They drank, both relaxing happily.

"So that's how you spend your time, Guy? Writing and flogging the occasional desirable property?"

He laughed. "More or less. But I do have other interests." Gill said nothing. He obviously wanted to tell her something. "Yes, I'm getting a bit involved politically."

"So?" she said.

"It's a bit hush-hush." He looked gravely at her. "If you don't mind, Gill?"

"I don't gossip."

"Right, well, a new grouping is being formed. In secret just for the moment. By people who are in favour of a truly Independent Scottish Parliament, but who can't agree fully with any of the main parties' current proposals."

"Fascinating," said Gill with unfeigned curiosity. "Where are the recruits coming from mainly? Right or Left?"

"Across the board. We've got disaffected Labourites, ex Lib-Dem people, SNP supporters who want a broader base, even some erstwhile Tory diehards." Guy spoke with enthusiasm.

"Have you a name yet?"

"Scottish Independence Group. S I G for short. It's a bit clumsy. It may be changed before our Charter is published."

"You've got that far?"

"Yes. The only thing that might spike our guns would be if one of the major parties suddenly swung right round to our point of view."

"Unlikely."

"I know, Gill, but it *could* happen."

"I suppose so."

Their main courses were delivered. After a few mouthfuls and mutual expressions of gastronomic pleasure Guy continued, "Whate'er betide, I'm hooked."

"Meaning?"

"Politics. I've been told there could even be an outside chance of standing as a Scottish Parliamentary candidate if the necessary constitutional changes occur. It's rather a thrilling idea, but a bit frightening too."

"Why frightening, Guy?"

"Well, lack of experience in government of any kind."

"I think a lot of people are going to have to learn on the job, fast, when the time comes."

"That's perfectly true of course, Gill. And, after all, I *have* studied the subject from the theoretical point of view at least. Machiavelli and all that! I wrote a rather good essay on old Niccolo at Oxford."

"'The Prince'. Yes. I'd say you're eminently qualified. As much as many are likely to be at the beginning anyway, Guy. We'll have to keep in touch. I'd like to know more about your new group too."

He reached over the table and took her hand. "Oh, Gill, I hope we shall."

She took her hand away. Now she must tell him. "Guy, I think there's something you maybe don't know about me."

"Yes?"

"I'm together with Willie Devine."

"I remember. The journalist chap. Yes, I did know you were friendly. Actually, I think he writes a lot of very good stuff."

"We're more than friends, Guy. I live with Willie." A vertical crease formed above his spectacles. "I hope you'll not be angry and that we can still be friends. Willie knows I'm here."

Guy Beaumont was a gentleman. Gill saw the struggle of annoyance and disappointment in his face, but he said, evenly, "I *didn't* know. That's quite right, Gill. But I'm flattered that nonetheless you accepted my invitation to meet."

"Can we stay friends, still meet?"

"Of course," said Guy, smiling charmingly once more.

And so it was to prove. Guy came through from Edinburgh quite often to see Gill. Soon after this first meeting her physical condition became noticeable, even to unobservant males: Guy took it in his stride. He obviously enjoyed her company and valued her opinions, especially on his developing political activities. Gill began to look forward to their outings. It was pleasant to chat and dine in smart places, escorted by an articulate, sophisticated man. He was always respectful of her commitment to Willie, who seemed just happy that she had found a good and politically sympathetic friend. She delighted in Willie's trust of her.

Willie obtained permission to see Lex Grant and Mo. The interviews didn't take long. Lex spent most of the time shouting obscenities. Incoherently he enjoined Willie to write articles of protest against the English, Westminster, the Labour Party in Scotland, the middle class leeches, the supine working class, the Church of Scotland lickspittles. It might have been almost funny if Willie hadn't detected an edge of derangement in the man's stream of indiscriminate condemnations. Lex was filled by hate, and here in jail there was no target for his vicious bile except thin air.

Mo Hossein was a pathetic sight. His prison clothes hung loosely about his slight frame. His hair had been cut very short. His skin colour was an odd greenish grey and his staring brown eyes seemed enormous. He recognized Willie with a slow nod, but thereafter was unwilling, or unable, to converse. Following several unsuccessful attempts to convey his sympathy and to enquire about Mo's living conditions, Willie gave up. It was only when he mentioned that he'd seen Mo's father and mother that there was a reaction: the gentle Pakistani broke into prolonged sobs until the guard led him away.

Willie stepped out of the grim building, profoundly saddened.

When he got home, there sat Hector Colquhoun with Gill. Willie's surprise was compounded by the Major's jumping up and levelling an imaginary shotgun at him.

"Here's the crack shot himself! How are you, Willie my boy?"

"All right, Major, thanks."

"Grandpa wanted to see us, Willie," said Gill "He rang earlier. I thought it'd be as good to chat here as anywhere?"

"Right. How did you get here?"

"Drove. Trusty old landrover. Gill's mother gave me your address."

"Where's the vehicle now?" asked Willie.

"Mr Gourlay, the janitor, is keeping an eye on it for me," said Gill. "It's parked in the school playground." She continued, "There's some tea here, Willie. Listen, I've a wee bit shopping to do so I'm going to leave you men to talk for a while. All right?"

Willie mumbled assent. He'd already guessed what this was about. They spoke briefly of the weather.

"The farmers are getting fed up with the wood-pigeons" said the Major. "They're having a big shoot soon. You know, straw bale hides, decoys. Rather a slaughter, no doubt, but necessary. I could get you invited if you'd like, Willie."

"Thanks, but I'm busy just now. Maybe not quite my scene anyway."

"No, perhaps not. Just a suggestion." He smiled indulgently.

Willie stood up. "I'll just pour myself a cup of tea."

"You carry on. Gill's filled me up already." The Major waited until Willie was seated again. "She was explaining to me about the date for the baby," he said with some deliberation.

"Uh-huh. The end of the year."

"Mid-November, I gather. Gill's mother was out at Dungearie the other day, Willie. She told me of her visit here." The Major had decided to say nothing to either of them about the probable divorce. He was a careful man and, after all, no papers had yet been signed.

"Oh yes? We don't see eye to eye, I'm sorry to say."

"Muriel's my only daughter, but that doesn't prevent me from being aware of her weaknesses. She's become a bit prickly in her middle age, rather intolerant. Nevertheless, she's not a fool, Willie. She's strong, particularly where family is concerned. Protective, you know. Perhaps women are a bit more like that than us?"

"There might be other ways of putting that."

"Yes, yes, I know. But let's not argue, Willie. I like to think we understand one another, you and I. The thing is, Muriel's looking ahead. When the time comes I expect she'll be over the moon to be a grandmother! It's the child, don't you see? She wants it to have the best possible start. No unnecessary handicaps."

Willie finished his tea. "You're talking about marriage, aren't you?"

"Of course." The Major waited expectantly.

"My experience of married couples has nearly all been negative. Especially RCs who can't easily divorce. Circumstances change, people change. Why suffer in a marriage that becomes a prison? Some folks live happily ever after of course. Good luck to them. What I ..."

"But, Willie ..." The Major interrupted.

Willie held up his hand. "Hear me out." The Major nodded. "I'm happy with Gill. She's a wonderful lassie and I love her. Probably I'd be content to end my days with her. But what about *her*? She might tire of yours truly. So I feel it's fairer to give her the right to an opt-out clause, without the hassle of a full-blown divorce." He rolled a cigarette, lit it, coughed, then inhaled deeply. "Anyhow, Gill's already my common-law wife, or soon will be. Also, I've had her entered in the *Recorder*'s pension scheme as my partner, my pregnant partner. If anything happens to me the scheme's trustees will see her right."

The Major absorbed all this. "You've clearly done everything you can to provide for Gill. I admire that. And you obviously care a lot about her, Willie. She certainly thinks the world of you. That kind of relationship is worth a very great deal." For a second or two he looked away thoughtfully. "But Willie, my friend, what about the baby's future? It's your child. Surely you wouldn't treat the baby with less care and affection?"

"The baby will be all right. The state doesn't discriminate nowadays."

The Major's smile faded. "I think the state's attitude is irrelevant, Willie. A family's pride matters, and that means observing the proprieties. If people make genuine mistakes, nowadays one doesn't react like the Victorians – ejecting them from society, cutting them out of wills etcetera. But that's on the basis that they *try* at least to play the game. D'you understand me?"

"I do, Major. You want us to get married."

"That's it, my boy! You're not really opposed, are you. After all, there's Gill's good name to remember too, Willie."

The prison visit had depressed Willie badly. He felt exhausted, unwell. He didn't want to argue any more. There was actually no need to decide anything at this moment. "I told Mrs MacIntyre we were thinking the matter over. Well, we are."

"Can't I take it you'll marry Gill, for the sake of her name and the baby, Willie? It's not as if you didn't get on. On the contrary ... so surely ... ?"

He didn't want to rebuff the old man. Willie liked him immensely. "I promise to decide soon, Major. Will that do?"

"It'll have to. Just remember your actions affect two other human beings directly, and several others indirectly." As a throwaway comment, he added "…and, I suppose, your own people."

"They couldn't care less," said Willie. "They're too busy keeping track of one another and making ends meet."

"I see. But your mother, Willie? She's alive?"

"Aye."

"Well, I'm sure she'll be glad to see you married and producing a grandchild."

"Last I heard she'd taken up with some man. And her with serious heart trouble too. I keep offering to go out to see her, but she tells me not to bother."

This finally silenced Hector Colquhoun. He'd done what he could. If he got a move on he might still catch that TV series on the Second World War.

"Very well, Willie. I'm sure you're going to do the right thing. Don't keep us waiting too long. Oh, and let me know when you'd like to come out to Dungearie again, when you're not in such demand by your paper." He stood up, patted Willie on the back, then shook hands warmly.

He had not been gone long when Gill returned.

"You been getting the third degree treatment, darling?" she enquired.

"Yes, but with velvet gloves."

"Grandpa really likes you, Willie. He made that clear when we had our chat earlier."

"Aye, well, it's mutual. He's a great character. Knows how to get his way."

"What d'you mean?"

"Och, nothing specific. He's just a persuasive bugger. Tenacious."

"Yes, well I don't suppose you can rise in the army and then finish up senior partner in a firm of stockbrokers unless you are fairly determined."

Willie made a gesture of agreement. "Of course you know why he was here?"

"Yes, I do, Willie. What did you say to him?"

"Same as I told your mother really. That we were considering the matter."

"And did he let it go at that?"

"He had to, in the end. But not before I'd had a lecture about family pride and he'd done some will-waving."

"He means well, Willie. I love him, more than my own parents, I think."

"I know," he replied quietly. Gill unpacked her shopping. After a time he said, "While we were talking I thought a lot. It almost seemed as if I were conducting a separate internal dialogue as I answered his questions. I came up with a surprising fact, Gill."

"What was that?"

"As near as I can enunciate it, it's this. All, or certainly for most of my adult life I've been fascinated by ... no, that's not honest. It's not strong enough. I've been *obsessed* by Scotland's completely unacceptable political position vis-à-vis the UK. All that. And I've always had a conviction that I, William Devine, could do something important to bring about constitutional change. Don't ask me where the arrogance springs from!"

"You're not arrogant, Willie. And you *are* doing something important."

"There's my champion!" He clasped his hands over his head in a victory salute. "Anyhow, as I say, this business has really dominated my whole life, consciously or unconsciously, for years. As long as I've been involved in work heading in the right direction, nothing else has seemed to matter much. I didn't bother with holidays, learning to drive, things like that."

"And women?"

He laughed. "Well, I hope I'm a normal male. I've had a few girlfriends. But that's the point I'm coming to, Gill. Till I met you, no relationship ever lasted. And I think it's because women have sensed that my life is, so to speak, 'on hold'. I mean, they could tell that I was serious enough, but about politics and Scotland's future, not about them. They realized I was a committed person, that I wouldn't change. So they moved on quickly." He shook his head, as if being compelled to acknowledge surprising things about himself. "I think I was usually relieved to be free of them to get on with my mission. Christ! *That* sounds arrogant! My 'mission'!"

"No it doesn't, Willie. And I do understand."

He smiled gratefully at her. "Well, I suppose what I'm trying to say, Gill, is that habits of mind like that die hard. As much as anything else, that's what's made me hesitate to talk about marriage. Us, I mean."

"It doesn't matter, Willie."

"But it does. There's a baby coming. In any case, you're not like the others. You're intelligently aware of Scotland's situation. You agree with my views. We can work together in the future, really help each other, Gill."

"Oh, Willie!"

They kissed passionately.

"Gill darling, will you marry me then?"

"Willie my darling darling! Yes I will."

They kissed again.

"I'm going to drink a bloody great whisky, even if you have to celebrate with fizzy water!"

Vaguely, still in a cocoon of excitement, they spoke of possible dates and venues. Eventually nothing was agreed except that the ceremony would be in a Registry Office, secular, private and soon.

Gill danced about preparing an evening meal. "Oh, I almost forgot!" She drew a letter from her handbag. "For you. I met the postman when I went out shopping."

Willie opened the envelope and read. His face darkened. It was from the Western Infirmary, with a copy to Dr McCabe. Willie was informed that the second x-ray tests had confirmed the almost certain presence of a tumour in his right lung. It would be necessary to operate and it was hoped that surgery could be confined to the affected pulmonary section but this could not be determined in advance. Would Mr Devine please ring the above number at the Gartnavel Hospital and make arrangements for an early admittance.

Wordlessly he handed the letter to his new fiancée.

# THIRTEEN

CATHIE LONIE AND SALLY Hughes stood as witnesses at the Registry Office. The four of them had a celebratory lunch at Luigi's Joint. But it was not easy to sustain the jollity the occasion merited: Willie was going into Gartnavel for his operation next morning.

Gill wrote to her parents and her grandfather to explain the situation. Muriel replied at once, outraged at the manner of the wedding and, especially, at her exclusion. She failed to mention Willie's health. Major Colquhoun congratulated Willie on winning a lovely bride, hoped Gill was taking good care of herself and was sure that Willie would soon be fit again. He felt that a short convalescent stay at Dungearie would do him a power of good.

Robert rang to wish them well and to ask Gill to have an early supper with him. He didn't comment on the unconventional nature of their wedding. They met two days later.

"Gill!" He embraced her. "It's been *ages*."

"It's good to see you, Dad."

"How's Willie? What's the news?"

"No news yet about how the operation's gone."

"But you've seen him?"

"Yes, but once only so far. He was too dopey to talk for more than a few minutes."

"Poor you. It's awful luck, coming at this time. I'm sure he'll be OK, but you need support."

"I'm fine, Dad, really."

"That's my brave Gill." He squeezed her hand.

Over the meal Robert informed his daughter, with difficulty, about the separation and the plans for eventual divorce. Gill was taken aback.

"So when will you leave Muirlaw Drive, Dad?"

"I did. Today."

"Heavens! I didn't realize ..."

"I'm sorry to hit you with this just now, Gill."

"No, it's all right. A shock but, well, where will you stay?" She looked at the so familiar face. "Won't you be lonely, Dad?"

"I'm at the Western Club for a few nights. After that I'll move to Kelvinside. Gill, you've met Lilias Watson, haven't you?"

"Your secretary? Yes ... I ..." Gill understood.

"Lilias and I are close. She's a dear woman, Gill. I need affection."

Gill smiled at him across the table. "Dad, I hope very much you'll be happy."

He returned her smile. "Please don't think I'm deserting your mother lightly. She'll be well provided for. I've done my best, Gill."

"My darling father, you've always done your best. There's no need to explain."

"Muriel's a good woman. She has fine qualities. But we don't agree, Gill. She's become hard. She can't accept different opinions from her own, different ways of approaching things."

"I know, I know. Especially where politics is concerned."

"Absolutely! We're at opposite poles!"

"I'm well aware of Mum's attitudes, Dad. Have you swung over to a Nationalist outlook then?"

"Oh I wouldn't say that!"

"But you're no Socialist or Lib-Dem."

"Certainly not."

"Then?"

"To tell you the truth, Gill, I just don't know. This whole business of Scotland's constitutional future, all the pros and cons – it's got me thoroughly bamboozled!"

"It can be confusing, I agree."

"Thank God, there's been no more violence. The prices of

Scottish-based companies have recovered. But that could easily be reversed. What's going to happen I've no idea. I haven't a crystal ball. I don't even know what I *think* should be done. I'm only a humble, hard-working businessman, Gill. All I want, really, is a quiet life. Quite honestly, politicians either disgust me or frighten me."

"Perfectly reasonable reactions, Dad!"


The surgeons did not remove a section of Willie's lung. Instead they carried out further extensive exploratory surgery. Heads were shaken and the afflicted body was simply sewn together again.

Inoperable cancer.

The phrase kept hammering in Gill's head. It was simply unbelievable, but, somehow, she had to bring herself to believe it. The doctors knew. They were experienced. They'd seen it all before. There was no possibility of a mistake. Willie was full of cancer and had between three and six months to live, with great luck perhaps nine.

Gill wept till she could weep no more. She visited the hospital twice a day until Willie came home. At first he seemed unchanged and carried on working normal hours, producing his column as before. But his cough and abdominal pains worsened by the week. Dr McCabe prescribed stronger pain-controlling tablets. He began to lose weight. His appetite was minimal. The doctors had told him he could continue smoking if he wished.

Towards the end of September his condition suddenly deteriorated. He ceased travelling to the office, wrote his copy at home and Gill posted it on her way to school. She had spoken to Sandy Black, the Editor, on the phone and he'd assured her that Willie would be paid right up to the end. He'd also mentioned that she would be taken good care of 'thereafter'.

Eventually Willie himself had to ring Black to advise him that he couldn't carry on. He spent longer periods in bed now, sometimes groaning piteously in pain. Gill's heart was broken. She quit school to nurse her dying husband. In any case, wee 'William Hector Devine' was beginning to assert himself forcibly – they were convinced that the child would be a boy. Just on the off-chance that they were surprised, however, a little girl would be plain Catherine.

Night after night, day after day, the agony went on. Despite chemotherapy Willie steadily declined. His hair began thinning. Cathie Lonie and Mrs Skelly sometimes relieved Gill for a few hours. Hector Colquhoun visited each week and was visibly upset. Robert came once.

Guy Beaumont was turning out to be a solid friend. He wrote regularly to Gill expressing sympathy and describing his increasing involvement with the new political group. She showed these letters to Willie. Guy and she met now and then. After one snatched evening, during which she'd cried a little from sheer exhaustion, he wrote to say how much he loved and admired her. He went on to say that if the worst were to happen she must remember that he was ready to comfort her and the baby. He fervently hoped that she would allow him that privilege. Indeed, he would consider it a high honour to be allowed to protect them both, formally, for the rest of his life. He believed he could have work to do in a new Scottish Administration, in some capacity, and he knew that Gill was totally in sympathy.

Gill did not give Willie that letter to read.

He still managed to get up each day for a while. Television no longer interested him but he listened a great deal to classical music on the radio.

"I feel I've missed a hell of a lot with music, Gill. Never had the time to listen properly somehow. This stuff's marvellous. Mind you, I can't make head nor tail of Bartok, or this Tippet guy. And this Scottish composer, James McMillan, is not easy either. But the older ones like Beethoven and Mozart and Tchaikovsky are great! Oh and Schubert and Bach. And Debussy too. Bloody terrific!"

Gill smiled at his unbounded enthusiasm. She had an idea.

"Willie, have you ever been to the Glasgow Concert Hall? You know, the new place?"

"No, I've never seen inside," he replied sadly.

"Would you like to go?"

"What?"

"You could make the effort, Willie. Sleep during the day. We'll stuff you with pills. A minicab both ways. I'll make sure it's a good programme. Really lush, romantic pieces. How about it?"

He was crying weakly. All he said was, "Gill, I love you."

She arranged it. They both knew it was their last outing.

"There's a Rachmaninov piano concerto in the first half, Willie. His number two in C minor. And a Mozart piece in the second half. I didn't recognize the pianist's name. Japanese, I think. Should be a lovely concert."

"Fabulous!"

The evening arrived. The minicab was waiting.

"Now, Willie, are you sure you're up to it?"

"I wouldn't miss this for anything."

"OK. Put on that old anorak of yours now."

"Och, I've got this thick pullover on."

"The anorak, Willie."

"Yes, Madam."

He complied with a grin on his haggard features.

In no time they were in the enormous modern foyer of the Concert Hall, pillarless and sumptuously carpeted. Then they were seated, programmes in hand, expectant.

The concert did not disappoint them. As the music majestically ebbed and flowed, the conductor maintained his overarching control, the pianist cleanly counterpointed her solo parts to the sweeping strings, the melodious woodwinds and brass. Willie was transported. Pain was forgotten for an hour. Gill observed his rapt, wasted face from the corner of her eye and wept inwardly.

Willie was determined to do things properly. He wanted to drink a whisky at one of the smart upstairs island bars, and he wanted too the pleasure of buying his wife a mineral water. They progressed slowly but eventually reached their objective and ordered drinks.

"Sorry but I'll have to go the Gents, Gill."

"It's all right, Willie. Just take your time. Don't hurry. I'll be waiting here for you, darling."

She looked around her. An interesting crowd promenaded about the spacious upper floor. A few bearded bejeaned student types but, in the main, concert-going Glasgow was decently accoutred. Dark suits, middle-price dresses, here and there a long skirt, a few elderly accountants or solicitors in kilts and tweed jackets. Gill felt warmly towards her fellow citizens.

"Well, I'll be buggered! It's Gill, isn't it?" Charlotte Cholmondley-Pickersgill was resplendent in a bare-shouldered low-cut black top and scarlet chiffon skirt.

"Oh, Charlotte! Hello. And Jamie."

The Beatties materialized. Both men wore evening dress.

"We go to supper after the concert, Gill. This is why we dress up, no?" said Maija Beattie. "And you? Not alone, I hope?"

"No, my husband's here. He'll be back in a minute."

"*Husband*?" said Jamie Ballantyne. "You mean...you married...?"

"Yes, some months ago. Willie Devine."

"Just in the *nick* of time, what?" Charlotte did her eye-rolling trick. "I've heard about your Willie. I'm looking forward to meeting him. He sounds *utterly terrifying*."

"He's been very ill, I'm, afraid."

"Sorry to hear that," said Alec Beattie.

There was an awkward pause. Charlotte said, "The four of us are off to sunny St Lucia next week. Should be fun."

"Lovely," said Gill. "I hope you enjoy it."

Then from the far side of the area there was Willie making his way painfully towards them. Over his arm he obediently carried his shabby old blue anorak. Even at a distance the lined pallor of his face was cruelly obvious under the brilliant concert hall lighting, as was the unhealthy condition of his tufty, sparse hair. He seemed small, shrunken. Gill fought back tears.

"Hello there," said Willie simply with a smile.

He was introduced to the three who had not met him before. They concealed their shock at his appearance. Except Maija. Her eyes moist, she patted Willie's forearm in consternation.

"You are not well, Willie. I'm so sorry ... poor man ... and poor Gill ... very sorry truly ... I ..."

"We'd better get back, I think," said Jamie rather too loudly. His embarrassment was palpable.

They moved away quickly. Gill shook her head with a sort of resigned anger. How miserably inadequate people could be in the face of others' distress.

"Och, you can't blame them, Gill," was Willie's comment. He then said, "Darling, I don't think I can last out the second half. I've enjoyed the music enough. It was glorious."

"Right. I prepaid the minicab, so it doesn't matter. Come on, we'll find a black taxi."

By the time they reached Rubyvale Street Willie was in agony. Somehow Gill got him upstairs and into bed. The taxi driver helped her. A burly young man, he was in tears as he left the flat: he knew very well who Willie Devine was.

A few pain-filled nights later Gill suddenly awoke. It was three thirty in the morning. She had recently become able to sleep through Willie's almost continuous groaning, but now, suddenly, all was quiet. She lay still, waiting for his tortured voice. There was no sound. In seconds she knew he was dead.


Over on the south side of the city in his trig new villa at Newton Mearns, Sandy Black put the finishing touches to Willie's obituary.

It had been frosty that Sunday morning, causing his bank manager friend, Lawson Dalziel, to call off their golf round. Sandy had enjoyed a lazy few hours with the papers before taking a snack lunch with Sheena, his wife – a tuna sandwich, a glass of Hungarian Riesling and a crisp Granny Smith apple. Then, in the afternoon, he'd raked up leaves from his front lawn and the garden's pathways, barrowing several loads up to the compost container behind the double garage. After that it was a warm, pump-assisted shower and an invigorating rub-down. Now, sitting comfortably before his word-processor in the study, he felt really braced up. Within his sky-blue towelling tracksuit his skin fairly tingled. His feet were snug in lambswool-lined deerskin moccasins.

Sandy checked through the obituary text on the screen one last time, then faxed the printout to the *Recorder* office. He'd be well inside the deadline for Monday's early edition.

A delicious spicy aroma reached his nostrils. Sheena was trying out a special fish stew recipe in the new Aga. He sauntered through to the kitchen, well pleased with himself, and gently slapped his wife's shapely behind. She turned round smiling and bestowed a brief kiss on his cheek. Maybe, thought Sandy, if she was still in a good mood after the meal he'd suggest they went to bed early.

"I've sent off the Devine article," he said. "Probably one of the best pieces I've ever written. Should take a trick or two."

### WILLIE DEVINE DIES

Willie Devine, 36, the well-known journalist who for the past three years has written a personal column for this newspaper, died at this home in Partick in the early hours of yesterday morning after a painful illness, bravely borne.

William McGrath Devine was born in 1959 into a family of five, living in humble circumstances in the Glasgow district of Partick, an area to which he was much attached and never left except on professional assignments.

Although his early years as a newspaperman were spent reporting and commenting in various fields, from sport to Royal Family matters, from arguments about Privatization issues to the attitude on terrorism of the Roman Catholic Church in Northern Ireland, Devine's overriding interest was always the political position of Scotland. From the very beginning his position was clear: a constitutional shake-up was overdue. A withdrawal from the 1707 Act of Union with England should be negotiated as soon as possible and an Independent Scottish Parliament set up in Edinburgh, elected by proportional representation with full powers in all areas such as taxation, social welfare and defence.

The *Glasgow Recorder* has been, and will remain, in full accord with those views.

It would be reasonable to conclude that Devine's politics were strictly in line with those of the Scottish National Party. But this would be to underestimate the breadth of the man's sympathies. He opposed the Conservatives' adherence to an inflexible United Kingdom structure administered centrally from Westminster. Equally, he considered the Labour and Liberal Democratic Parties' proposals for a Devolved Scottish Assembly with limited authority, and ultimately subservient to Whitehall and the Westminster Government, to be unworkable.

The *Recorder* has always backed Devine in those rejections.

What he advocated was that all the main political parties in Scotland try to sink their differences and work jointly for the negotiation of Independence. This would of course be a totally peaceful process. Devine was emphatic in his condemnation of violence on the IRA pattern, or indeed as occurred so tragically in George Square, Glasgow, earlier this year.

Once the arrangements for an Assembly were

in place, Devine had implicit faith in the good sense of the Scottish people to elect a Parliament which would fairly reflect all strands of political opinion in the country. On the face of it this might initially mean an overwhelmingly Socialist or Nationalist Administration, but Devine always maintained that neither was a foregone conclusion. He was mindful of traditionally differing attitudes in the North East and the Borders from those prevalent in the Central Industrial belt or the Western Highlands. He commended the patient work of the Scottish Constitutional Convention to devise a system of franchise which will ensure no one party dominates unreasonably.

With this fundamental trust in the Scottish people to run their own affairs efficiently and democratically The *Recorder*, once again, endorses Devine's opinions.

He was no bigot, no simplistic anglophobe. Willie Devine was a true patriot and, in the traditions of this newspaper, free from narrow party bias, dedicated only to his country's welfare. He passionately wanted Scotland to recover her self-confidence, her dignity, her Independence as a nation state, conscious of her illustrious history but looking also to the future as an active, participating member of the European Community and Parliament in her own right.

Following a sensible settlement with Westminster, he believed that more than adequate financial resources would be available to tackle the many serious social problems that exist in this country. The favourable offset of increased North Sea Oil taxation revenues against the cut-off of current Central Government transfers, and the huge savings which would accrue to Scotland as a result of withdrawal from the Trident Nuclear Submarine project would be two of the main sources of additional income to the Scottish Treasury. And with the hands-on ability to offer tax incentives, Scotland could well attract considerably more investment by overseas industrial giants in the future than she already enjoys.

Recent opinion poll findings indicate a burgeoning support throughout Scotland for the cause courageously espoused for so long by Devine. The *Glasgow Recorder* is proud to continue the fight. There is talk in Press circles of the striking of a Devine Medal, to be awarded each year to the journalist who has done most to advance the interests of Scotland. We will support this initiative.

But the best memorial to Willie Devine will be the birth of a truly Independent Scotland in the not too distant future, a nation which is likely to be a much more comfortable and co-operative neighbour than at present.

We extend our deepest sympathy to his wife, Gillian, who is expecting their first child next month.

The rest of the Scottish Press, followed by the London papers, paid similar tributes to Willie's work and reputation. Many did not agree with his views on the best course for Scotland – although their alternative positions often sounded stale, confused – but all praised his disinterested single-mindedness and regretted his untimely death. As one writer put it: 'Scotland is a small country. At this time she desperately needs the few Willie Devines she possesses'.

Gill collected all the obituaries. Wee William, or Catherine, would be proud to read them one day. Now it was Wednesday. She had the cremation to face on Friday.

Guy Beaumont was going to take her in his car to the funeral but he wanted to see her first.

"Gill, I hope you don't mind."

"Come in, Guy. I'm pleased to have your company."

She made tea.

"Driving through, I was thinking of what all those obituaries have said. I'm glad you insisted on bringing me here the other week. He was certainly a special person."

"He was, Guy."

"I just wish, in a way anyway, I'd had a chance to know him before he got so ill."

Gill smiled faintly. "Willie told me he liked you, Guy. He even said he was glad I had met you. I think he guessed we were fond of one another."

Guy swallowed. "Christ! That was generous."

"He was like that."

He put his arm round her. "I don't know if I can live up to that standard, Gill. I don't know if I'm good enough."

"You're an honest and worthwhile man, Guy dear. You're certainly as good a person as I'll ever be." She kissed him briefly on the lips. "Maybe people like Willie are just not allowed to live long lives."

"You'll need some time to get over all this, Gill, and to have your baby. But, unless you stop me, I'm hoping to visit you nearly every day."

"I won't stop you."

"Then, when you've recovered, we'll decide our plans." Suddenly he looked anxious. "I'm not pushing you, Gill, am I? I mean, the funeral hasn't taken place yet and here am I ..."

"It's all right, Guy. You're not pushing me at all."

"Oh, OK then. Well, I hope you can sleep tonight, darling Gill. I'll be back for you at eleven tomorrow morning."

"Good night, Guy. Take care on the road."

They arrived early at the crematorium. There seemed to be a crowd gathering at the gates and Guy was forced to sound his horn to clear a way through. Inside, the building was empty except for an elderly official who guided them to the front pews. Guy took his place just behind Gill. Recorded secular organ music came from somewhere in the bare walls.

Robert was the first to come in. He sat beside Gill. She introduced Guy. Then two women walked down to the front.

"You Gill? Willie's Gill?"

"Yes, that's right."

"Uh-huh. We're Willie's sisters. I'm Betty and this is Mina."

The first woman was rather fat, the other tallish with the traces of freckles on her face.

Mina said, "Mither couldnae come wi' her heart. We couldnae contact our brithers. One's down in England somewhere. Charlie's on holiday in Majorca. Package, like, so he couldnae make it either."

"It's good of you to come anyway."

"Och, dinnae mention it, hen."

They sat down on the opposite pew.

Then Hector Colquhoun arrived. He sat on Gill's other side.

"This is a sad, sad day, my dear girl," he whispered. "Just bear up for now, there's a brave lass. Here, hold my hand."

She did so. "Thank you, Grandpa," she murmured.

Sandy Black and some *Recorder* colleagues came in, paid their respects and sat down. Then Hamish MacCorquodale appeared, all windblown red hair and glasses. He came to Gill. She could see the tears in his eyes.

"Ah, Chillian, Chillian," he began, but could not continue. "I ... I'll see you afterwards, outside."

A number of well-dressed men and a severe pin-striped woman filed in. Gill glanced round but didn't know any. Then she noticed Sandy Black greeting them, each by name: editors and journalists from other newspapers. She felt a surge of pride.

The back pews were full now. Some poorly dressed individuals she recognized as regulars from the Argyle. One she thought she knew the name of – Jumpie MacPherson. The others must have been ordinary people, from Partick probably. A sniffing Mrs Skelly sat behind with Guy. They'd given her a lift. Her head was reverently covered with a black headscarf.

It was almost time. Then Muriel's high heels tapped down the aisle. She wore a new black hat and coat.

"Darling! I'm so sorry. Are you all right ... Can I ..."

"I'm all right, Mum."

"Sit down, Muriel," commanded Robert. And she did, on his other side from Gill.

Very quickly the non-religious ceremony was over. Willie had insisted it be like this. No fuss. The formal platitudes went over Gill's head, but then the curtains parted and the coffin began to roll out of sight. The undertakers' representative said: "Relatives and friends of the deceased, today we say farewell to William Devine. Let us remember his life and work as we commit his body to the elements whence it came, to be consumed by fire."

The dam of Gill's suffering finally broke. She sobbed without restraint. The Major cradled her in his arms. Robert patted her knee constantly. Guy leant forward and kissed the top of her head, his glasses removed, tears running down his face.

Mrs Skelly was undone. "Ah, dinnae greet sae sair, lassie! Aw, ma darlin' wee Gill ... dinnae greet, lambie. Aw God! ... puir Willie ... It's no fair ... Och, Gill, dinnae greet!"

Many others were affected. They were all identified, in greater or lesser degree, with Scotland and her future. Willie Devine and all he'd stood for, all the troubling, perplexing questions he'd raised so often, so fearlessly, and for so long – he and they were a part of them too. Gill's loss was also theirs.

Outside a smirr had set in. Hamish told her he was soon leaving for Nova Scotia to collect Gaelic material for a Canadian TV documentary. Sandy Black asked her to come to his office as soon as she felt able, to tie up the pension arrangements. Jumpie MacPherson took off his bunnet, revealing an unexpected expanse of bald pate, and pumped her hand, saying that Willie Devine was his best friend and the finest man he'd ever met.

Muriel told Gill she mustn't hesitate to call on her if she needed help with the baby. Gill looked her in the eye unsmilingly.

"I expect I'll manage, Mum," she said and turned away.

The Major gave her a final hug. Robert kissed her and said he'd be in touch soon, that Lilias wanted to meet her properly.

It was over. Then Jumpie appeared again.

"Hiv ye seen the gang at the gate yonder? Hunners o' them! Wi' notices on sticks an' that. Willie would have bin pleased, so he would."

Guy and Gill walked a short distance down the tarmac drive. Beyond the railings there was indeed a large crowd of demonstrators. 'Free Scotland Now!', 'Grant a Scottish Parliament', 'Independence not Devolution!', read their placards. One said, 'Remember Willie Devine'. Two mounted police had already arrived, their batons unsheathed.

Gill had another cry, but she was under control now. Guy put his arm round her waist. They collected Mrs Skelly and were soon on their way back.

Cathie Lonie had not attended the funeral. Instead, she was waiting for them at Rubyvale Street with sherry and coffee, a tray of freshly made sandwiches and a custard trifle.

By three in the afternoon they had no more to say to one another. Mrs Skelly and Cathie left. Guy embraced Gill tenderly, assuring her that he'd phone next day, that he wanted to be closely in touch.

"In fact, that's what I want for the rest of my days, my darling darling Gill."


Major Hector Colquhoun returned to Dungearie sad but angry at the same time. The misery of the occasion had been bad enough, but the added blight of Muriel's alienation from her husband and pregnant daughter had seemed unbearable.

Mrs Campbell ushered him into the hall. "Och, Major, you must be wore out. Funerals is awful. Now, I've got a nice mince tart ready. It'll put some heart back into you."

"Thank you, Margaret. I'll just get out of this suit first. I could do with a brandy and soda, if you'd be so kind."

"It'll be ready when you come down."

After his meal he felt slightly better, but the wretchedness of the morning still clung. He tried to read the paper but couldn't concentrate. About three he stood up and looked out of the window. The rain had cleared. There was even a blink of sun between high clouds. He decided to take a walk.

"Aye, that's just the thing, Major. A blow'll do you good." Mrs Campbell handed him his deerstalker and his stick.

He called Gypsy to heel and set off. There was a breeze now, so he walked briskly. Gill kept coming into his mind. Her abject sorrow as she'd sobbed in his arms had pierced his heart. How unfair a hand she'd been dealt. Still, she was a darling, plucky girl. She'd recover and be a good mother. He'd keep a close eye on her. And that young man from Edinburgh had seemed very devoted, so perhaps she'd marry again before too long.

Then Willie was there beside him again. It was as yesterday that they'd talked politics and then walked out this way. How well the pair of them had got on. Of course the man had been shy at first, suspicious even, but it had been rewarding to draw him out, to see his confidence grow, to get him laughing easily. He had courage though and no lack of brains. Many of the arguments Willie had made for constitutional change in Scotland had been convincing. He'd been forced to give them a very great deal of thought. Indeed, the Major felt that it would not be an exaggeration to say that Willie Devine had turned him into an enthusiast for a properly established Scottish Parliament. It had not been so much a conversion which had occurred as a reawakening, a buttressing of his underlying, wholly natural pride in his country. He was going to miss Willie badly. Differences of class and religious background had fallen away when they were together.

There was something deeper in the Major's sense of desolation. He'd always wanted a son. Ever since the complications at Muriel's birth it had been out of the question and he'd stoically accepted the fact. Most of the time he'd kept it out of his mind, but sometimes when he was in the presence of colleagues' or friends' boys he'd felt it. Or when others spoke of their sons' academic progress or sporting achievements. Or when they took them into their businesses. Robert McIntyre was a good fellow and, as far as he could remember, they'd never had a cross word. But he was absolutely conformist, not tough-minded or idealistic, like Willie.

He came to the place of rushes where he'd taught Willie to use a 12 bore. Uncannily he could feel again the bony shoulders through the anorak as he'd helped him straighten his aim. The Major was suddenly overcome by a corroding sense of hopeless grief. He was old now. Willie had meant vigour, boldness and, above all, a selfless dedication to the future of Scotland. At that moment Hector Colquhoun admitted to himself that he'd begun to love Willie as a son.

He stopped in his tracks and looked up through tears at the banked clouds. A terrible cry of anguish was dragged from his strong chest: "Aaaaaaah ... Willie! Willie!" There was a brief muffled echo. Gypsy crouched, her staring eyes wide with puzzlement at the strange sound from her master. The Major bent down immediately and stroked her silky head. "Never mind, Gypsy," he said hoarsely "you and I will just have to go on, won't we?"

He remained where he was for a few minutes. To the East, not far away, was the field of Bannockburn with its massive statue of The Bruce on his warhorse. Further north atop Abbey Craig near Stirling was the monument to Sir William Wallace. What would those past champions of Scotland's nationhood make of the country's situation today? Of course it was a childishly romantic thought but, then again, Willie Devine was no childish romantic. Far from it. For Major Colquhoun, Willie was a fighter to be ranked honourably with those ancient Scottish heroes. But would his efforts, and the strivings today of all the others of like mind, be as gloriously rewarded? These constitutional questions had to be decided, and soon. Otherwise the people of Scotland, especially the young, could become irredeemably cynical.

He sighed heavily. On the Fintry hilltops the season's first dusting of snow showed faintly pink in the declining sun's rays. The breeze was stiffening to a steady wind now. It was cold on the back of his neck as he whistled for Gypsy and started home. There was a definite change in the weather coming.